3/97

A COMPREHENSIVE DICTIONARY OF THE GODS

A COMPREHENSIVE DICTIONARY OF THE GODS

ANNE S. BAUMGARTNER

WINGS BOOKS
New York • Avenel, New Jersey

This 1995 edition is published by Wings Books,
distributed by Random House Value Publishing, Inc.,
40 Engelhard Avenue, Avenel, New Jersey 07001,
by arrangement with Carol Publishing Group.

Random House
New York • Toronto • London • Sydney • Auckland

Printed and bound in the United States of America

Library of Congress Cataloging–in–Publication Data

Baumgartner, Anne S.
    [Ye gods!]
    A comprehensive dictionary of the gods / Anne S. Baumgartner.
        p.   cm.
    Originally published: Ye gods! New York : Carol pub., 1984.
    ISBN 0–517–12358–4 (hardcover)
    1. Mythology—Dictionaries.   I. Title.
BL473.B36   1995   95–30169
291.2'11'03—dc20   CIP

8   7   6   5   4   3   2   1

I dedicate this book to my parents, Norbert C. Scherger (deceased) and Mary G. Scherger. They have my deepest love, gratitude, admiration and respect. They believed in me, taught me to question and to laugh, and loved me even when I tried their patience. Believe me, I did try their patience. Mom, have I ever apologized for that?

And, also, to my husband Gary. Thanks for all that boundless faith in one pint-sized mortal female.

FOREWORD

Mythology does not have to be a dull subject. In fact, it shouldn't be. Humankind is a lusty, brawling race that delights in challenge. Its gods, for the most part, have been no different. To their believers, these gods of old were truly superhuman in the sense that they far exceeded normal beings in every way.

Zeus is an excellent example. Much has been written of this kingly Olympian god's great powers, but there are some who would like to forget his 115 mistresses and 140 (at last count) children. To such people, it somehow doesn't seem proper for a god to be so lusty a being. Obviously, the Greeks didn't agree.

7

To our ancestors, the old gods and goddesses were anything but dull. Kubaba, goddess of ancient Kish, started off as a barmaid. It's not an unusual calling when you realize that strong drink was regarded by many people as a gift of the gods. That might help explain why wise old Silenus stayed drunk most of the time.

Far too often, mythological beings are viewed through glasses grown dim with the dust of ages and blurred by smudges of religious and social prejudice. There are other kinds of preconceived notions as well. Scientists, supposed objective observers, will readily admit that dinosaurs existed. Dragons, however, are quite another matter. And while they have come around to the idea that continents can float, they haven't yet admitted that one might sink.

This book is an attempt to blow away some dust and wipe up smudges. Along the way, it provides a little humor to leaven the heavy mass of learning. The gods don't mind laughter at all. In fact, there is strong evidence to indicate that they invented it.

CONTENTS

ABBREVIATIONS

abbr.—abbreviation
aka—also known as
dba—doing business as
pseud.—pseudonym
qv—which see (or *quod vide*)

I

ABAASY TO AZI WITH AN ASIDE ON THE AMESHA SPENTAS

ABAASY—*Yakut tribe*
A race of netherworld inhabitants with teeth of iron. They appear to travel in packs of seven or so.

ABELLO—*Gaul*
God of apple trees.

ABNOBA—*Gaul*
Goddess of the Black Forest.

ACHELOUS—*Greek*

Son of Oceanus and Tethys. Most celebrated of the river gods. As befitting a divine being of his stature, he was endowed with a serpentlike body and horned head. He became enamoured of the maiden Deianeira. Unfortunately, the upstart mortal Herakles also had designs upon her. In the ensuring confrontation, Herakles tore off one of Achelous's horns. The nymphs fashioned this into the Horn of Plenty.

ADITI—*India*

Mother of gods, Mother of worlds, Infinite Light and protectress and leader of mortals.

ADLIVUN—*Eskimo*

The abode of Sedna, goddess of the sea. This is the place where the dead are purified before continuing their journey to the Land of the Moon.

AEGIR—*German*

Husband of Ran. Aegir is god and master of the sea. He is known for the lavish entertainments he gives for the other gods. His wife Ran sinks ships in storms and then tenderly ministers to the drowned sailors. You see, Ran has nine daughters of marriageable age.

AESIR—*German*

Odin, Thor, Balder, Freyr, Tyr, Bragi, Hodr, Heimdall, Vithar, Vali, Ullr, Ve and Forseti—collectively. This group of gods resides in Asgard and their home is called Gladsheim. At one time, they warred with a rival group of gods called the Vanir. However, hostilities have since ceased and both groups are now good friends.

AEOLUS—*Greek*

A mortal whom Zeus made ruler of the winds. Aeolus has the winds bagged and stored in various caves. He releases them when the gods instruct him to do so.

AETHER—*Greek*

Son of Erebus and Nox. The god of clear skies.

AFREET—*Arabic*

Unclean spirits.

AGNI—*India*

God of lightning, fire and the sun. He is also the mediator between humans and the gods. He is the gentlest of the gods and those who know him ascribe this trait to the fact that he is the only fire god who was born in the water. Agni is also known as Pavaka, Dhumaketu, Jatavedas and Anala. He is one of the few guides mortals can trust, for he is the Master of the Universe.

AGUARA—*Tunpa and Chiriguano Indians*

The fox-god who gave humans the carob tree.

AHRIMAN—*aka* Angra Mainyu—*Persia*

Son of Zurvan. The evil one who opposes Ohrmazd. *dba* Ahura Mazda.

AHURA MAZDA—*Persia*

Son of Zurvan. Supreme god. Lord and Creator. You may have noted his symbol from time to time. It is the winged disc.

AITVARAS—*Prussia*

Aitvaras is a brave and loving demon. He will bring good fortune to your house if he is fed well and treated kindly.

AIZEN-MYOO—*Japan*

God of love, prostitutes, singers, tavern-keepers and musicians. If you do not understand how this can be, you will never know as much about love as the Japanese do.

AJBIT—*Maya*

One of the 13 gods who created human beings. Ajbit assisted in the actual construction work.

AJTZAK—*Maya*

He did the same thing as Ajbit did. There's a lot of repetitive work in building mortals.

AJYSYT—*Yakut (Siberia)*

The goddess of children and laughter and nations. She protects women in childbirth.

AL BORAK—*Arabian*

The winged white mare who bore the Great Prophet Mohammed from Earth to Seventh Heaven.

ALALUS—*Hurrite*

Reigned as King of Heaven for nine years until he was deposed by Anus. Upon leaving the heavenly throne, Alalus descended to Earth where he was fed by Kumarbis, father of the gods.

ALASTOR—*Greek*

He began existence as a mortal, the son of Neleus, King of Pylos. Alastor and many of his brothers were slain by Herakles. After his untimely death, Alastor became a minor spirit who avenged evil deeds and demanded vengeance for crimes.

ALFS—*Germanic*

A minor race of gods.

ALIGNAK—*Eskimo*

God of the moon, governor of the falling snow, storms, eclipses, earthquakes and tides. Protector of orphans, animals and the disinherited. A needful ward against the mighty anger of Sedna, goddess of the sea. When predisposed to do so, he can cure sterility in women.

ALOADAE—*aka* Aloidae—*Greek*

Otus and Ephialtes, the twin sons of Poseidon and Iphimedia. By the time they had attained the age of nine, they were each 54 feet tall. This gave rise to some delusions on their part and they wished to wage war with the other gods. In order to reach the gods, Otus and Ephialtes began piling mountains on top of each other. This did the surrounding landscape no good at all and caused something of a commotion. The matter came to the attention of Apollo, who destroyed them.

ALOM—*Maya*

God of the sky. One of the seven gods who assisted in the creation of the world and also of humans.

ALPHEUS—*Greek*

A river god who fell in love with the delightful nymph Arethusa as she bathed in his waters. Artemis did not approve of the union and took it upon herself to change Arethusa into a fountain and move her to Syracuse. Alpheus, much annoyed, dived underground and emerged in Syracuse, where he mingled his waters with those of his beloved.

AMA no UZUME—*Japanese*

The witty and clever goddess of persuasion. When the sun goddess Amaterasu went and hid

herself in a cavern, none could talk her into coming
out. Ama no Uzume began to perform a most lewd
dance which made the gods rock with laughter.
Amaterasu became so curious that she could no
longer stand it and came out of the cavern to see what
was going on.

AMAETHON—*Celtic*
Son of Dana and Beli. God of agriculture.

AMAGANDAR—*aka* Orokannar—*Tungus*
Female spirits of protection.

AMATERASU—*Japanese*
The sun goddess. Humans love and respect her a
good deal because she aids them in their constant
battle to sustain themselves. She is the ruler of the
Plain of Heaven and the sister of the storm god
Susanowo.

AMBARVALIA—*Roman*
The festival of Ceres (*qv*), held in May.

AMESHA SPENTAS—*Persia*
Powerful immortals. They are gods without
being gods and created without being creatures. The
six Amesha Spentas are properly titled Yazata, which
is a term of respect. Their names are: Vohu Manah,
Kshathra, Asha, Amererat, Haurvatat and Armati.

VOHU MANAH takes the souls of the just to
Paradise.

KSHATHRA is the defender of the poor even
though he would rather defend royalty. He is a great
warrior who uses his weapons to maintain peace.

ASHA protects the physical and moral order of
the world. It is his task to be the principal adversary
of the world of the demons.

ARMATI, the ancient and wise patroness of the earth, appears devoted, adoring and submissive. Submission can be most deceptive at times.

HAURVATAT and AMERETAT are the aides of Armati. Haurvatat brings prosperity and health and Ameretat brings immortality.

AMMA—*Dogon of the Sudan*

Father of Yurugu and the twins called Nommo. Supreme god. God of fertility. God of rain.

AMON—*aka* Amon-Re, Amun, Niu and Amun-Re— *Egyptian*

Husband of Mut, father of Khons, the moon god. God of mystery (see ISLAND OF FLAME), god of healing, god of justice, god of the welfare of the state in peace and war. Became king of the gods through the actions of mortals. When the god Month fell into disfavor with the human princes of Egypt's Eleventh Dynasty, they adopted Amon as the god of the royal residence. Once installed in the palace, his rapid rise to the King of Heaven and chief god of Egypt was breathtakingly clever.

AMPHITRITE—*Greek*

Sea goddess. She is either the daughter of Oceanus and Tethys or of Nereus and Doris. Amphitrite says she does not remember and neither does anyone else. However, she is the wife of Poseidon and the mother of Triton, himself a sea god. Amphitrite gets along well with dolphins, although this was not always the case. When Poseidon wanted Amphitrite for his bride, she declined the honor and hid. Poseidon sent a dolphin to find her. The dolphin not only located Amphitrite, he delivered her to

Poseidon. Amphitrite was annoyed. Poseidon awarded the dolphin a place in heaven.

AMPHION—*Greek*

Son of the God Zeus and Antiope, princess of Thebes. Twin brother of Zethus. When but a child, Amphion was taught to sing and play the lyre by Hermes. Being a true son of Zeus, his charmed music was such that it caused stones to form themselves into walls and that is why Thebes had such magnificent walls at one time.

AMUNET—*aka* Niut—*Egyptian*

Goddess of Mystery. For more details, see Is-LAND OF FLAME.

AN—*Sumer*

High god of heaven.

ANAITIS—*Asia Minor*

Goddess of immortality and fertility. The goddess who presides over the waters.

ANANSE—*Ashanti, Africa*

Son of Asase Ya and Nyame. Creator of the sun, moon, stars, day and night. He often intercedes between gods and mortals and aided mortals by giving them the first grain. He also set himself up as the first king of the human beings.

ANANTA—*India*

The principle of omnipresence and extension.

ANAT—*Ugarit*

Sister of Baal. Goddess of life and fertility. The warrior virgin and slayer of serpents.

ANDARTA—*Gaul*
Warrior goddess.

ANDRASTA—*Gaul*
Another warrior goddess.

ANDRIANAHOABU—*Madagascar*
A member of the Zankary family of gods. She is the Lady on High who descends to Earth on a silver chain.

ANDRIANAMBOATENA—*Madagascar*
Another member of the Zankary family. He is the god of Earth.

ANDRIAMANITRA and ANDRIANAHARY—*Madagascar*
Good and even gods who created the earth and the tribe of mortals.

ANDVARI—*Scandinavia*
A dwarf who amuses himself by turning into a fish and living in the water.

ANGEKKOKS—*Eskimo*
Priests.

ANGELS
These spirits act as messengers between Heaven and Earth. There are nine orders of angels at present. They are: Seraphim, Cherubim, Thrones, Dominations, Principalities, Powers, Virtues, Archangels and Angels. Humans rarely come into contact with any but the lowest order, which is the one assigned to human affairs, and this is why humans describe this spirit family simply as Angels. It is not known if angels accept such assignment with humility.

ANNWN—*Celtic*
The Kingdom of the Dead.

ANSHUR—*aka* Ashur and Asshur—*Assyrian*
God of the sun. It was he who was victorious over the Dragon of Chaos during the great work of Creation.

ANTAEUS—*Greek*
Son of Poseidon and Gaea. Antaeus was the King of Libya and a giant of great strength. He was proud of his skill as a wrestler and remained unbeaten until Herakles challenged him to a match and crushed him to death. It was a most ungracious act.

ANTI—*Egypt*
The god of ferrymen.

ANU—*Babylon*
God of heaven, god of storms and winds, god of the waves.

ANUBIS—*Egypt*
Son of Osiris. Judge and protector of the dead and therefore god of the dead and of embalming. Protector of tombs. It was he who instigated the practice of weighing the hearts of the dead against the Feather of Truth.

ANUNNAKI—*Sumer*
The assembly of the high gods. When they decided to destroy humankind with a great flood, Ziusudra, King of Shurappak, was forewarned of the deluge. He built an ark in which the seeds of the mortals were preserved during the seven days and seven nights the waters raged.

ANUS—*Hurrite*

He ruled as King of Heaven for nine years. Not content with this, he declared war on the father of the gods, Kumarbis. Anus lost and fled through the skies and stars. By the time Kumarbis finally captured Anus he was so irritated that he castrated the former king. Anus has been hiding ever since.

ANZETY—*Egypt*

God and king of Busiris.

APHRODITE PANDEMOS—*Greek*

Daughter of Uranus. Mother of Eros, Anteros, Deimus, Phobus and Harmonia, by Ares. Goddess of sex, often referred to archly as "common love."

APIS—*Egypt*

A sacred bull which Osiris sent to mortals as his representative. An apis was recognized by his black hide, triangle of white on the forehead, white crescent spot on the right side and a knot under his tongue. Each apis was venerated by the priests who gave him food and shelter and then slew him when he reached his 25th year. This explains why Osiris sent representatives to deal with humans. At last report, Osiris was no longer even doing that.

APOLLO—*Greek*

Son of Zeus and Leto. Twin brother of Artemis. Father of Asclepius by the mortal female Coronis. Apollo's hair has a curious blue tinge which many find remarkable. He is the god of light, sun, archery, agriculture, animal husbandry, crops, cattle, farmers, shepherds, sheep, poetry, song, healing, medicine, physicians, prophecy, morality, ethics and several other things. He is the founder of cities, giver of laws, purifier of contrite wrongdoers and punisher of those guilty of overweening pride.

APOPHIS—*Egypt*
The demon of darkness.

APOTHEOSIS—*Greek*
The Greek gods deified some mortals after those mortals died. Since many of the humans who were apotheosized were rulers of cities and states, other cultures assumed that anybody who ruled did so by divine right. This foolish assumption led to disastrous results.

APSU—*Sumer*
The primeval abyss.

ARAZU—*Babylon*
The god of completed construction.

ARDUINNA—*Gaul*
The goddess who rules the Ardennes.

ARDVI SURA ANAHITA—*aka* Anahita—*Persia*
The goddess of rivers and water.

ARES—*Greek*
Son of Zeus and Hera. The big love of his life was Aphrodite, although he wasn't exactly what you would call a one-woman man. All of his sons came to bad ends because they were bloodthirsty dolts. However, his daughters, the Amazons, were greatly respected by all.

ARIADNE—*Greek*
A mortal. Daughter of Minos, king of Crete. Wife of Bacchus. She helped her lover Theseus kill the

Minotaur in the Labyrinth beneath her father's palace in Knossos. Theseus, expressing the gratitude common among mortal males, took Ariadne with him when he fled, then abandoned her on the island of Naxos. This was where Bacchus found her and married her.

ARIANROD—*Celtic*
Only daughter of Dana and Beli. Mother of Lleu, or Llew, by Gwydion. Goddess of the moon.

ARINNA—*Hittite*
Goddess of the sun.

ARISTAEUS—*Greek*
Son of Apollo and the nymph Cyrene. Protector of flocks. It was he who originated the culture of the olives.

ARTEMIS—*Greek*
Daughter of Zeus and Leto. Twin sister of Apollo. Goddess of the moon and the hunt. The virgin goddess who assists in childbirth and protects the young of animals and humans. Patron of the Amazons.

ARTIO—*Scandinavian*
The goddess of bears.

ASASE YA—*Ashanti, Africa*
Wife of Nyame. Mother of the gods.

ASCLEPIUS—*aka* Aesculapius—*Greek*
Son of Apollo and Coronis, a mortal, who was the daughter of King Phlegyas of Thessaly. A talented lad who was taught medicine by Chiron the Centaur. So well did he learn it that he was able to raise the dead.

ASHERA—*Phoenician*
   Goddess of fertility.

ASHNAN—*Sumer*
   Goddess of grain.

ASIAQ—*Eskimo*
   Goddess of the weather.

ASTARTE—*Semite*
   (Semite, in case you do not know, refers to
Phoenicians, Babylonians, Assyrians, Carthegenians,
Egyptians, Canaanites and other civilized people.)
Goddess of love, battle, war, sex, fertility and mater-
nity. It is a matter of proud tradition among the many
who worship Astarte that the mother of the tribe
leads the tribe in battle.

ASTRAEA—*Greek*
   Daughter of Zeus and Themis. Goddess of justice. She was a regular inhabitant of the earth at one
time, but she fled to the skies when mortals began
making war.

ASVINS, DASRA and NASATYA—*India*
   Husbands of Surya, daughter of the sun god.
They are the twin gods of light. They cure all
infirmities.

ATAR—*Persia*
   God of all fire.

ATARGATIS—*Syria*
   Goddess of fertility and of nature. She is believed
to be the founding mother of the mermaids, as she is
a most beautiful woman with the tail of a fish.

ATHIRAT—*Ugarit*

Official wife of El, the Supreme God. Widely known as Athirat the Merciful.

ATLANTIS

An island empire which was the site of the Fountain of Youth. It was destroyed in the process of continental drift.

ATE—*Greek*

Daughter of Zeus. Goddess of discord and mischief. Her sisters, the Litai, follow her around picking up the pieces and repairing the damage Ate has wrought to mortals.

ATEN—*Egypt*

God of the sun, light, providence and life.

ATHENA—*Greek*

Daughter of Zeus and Metis. Goddess of war, wisdom, industry, the arts, justice and skill. The inventor of sailing ships and chariots. She is also the virgin mother of Erichthonius, whom she loves.

ATLAS—*Greek*

Son of Iapetus and Clymene. Brother of Menoetius, Prometheus and Epimetheus. A Titan who took part in the rebellion against Uranus. Zeus punished him for this by making him hold up the sky forever.

ATMA—*India*

The divine spark in mortals.

ATUGAN—*Mongolia*

Goddess of Earth and source of all life. The power of Atugan is beyond understanding and can be bestowed.

ATUM—*Egypt*
Son of Nun. Father of Shu and Tefnut by self-fertilization. First born of the gods.

AUDHUMLA—*German*
The cow created from the melted waters of Eternal Ice and given life by the Fiery Wind of the southlands. She created Buri who, in turn, created his son Bor. The milk from Audhumla's udders fed the Giant Ymir when there was naught else to eat.

AUDJAL—*Caroline Islands*
Earth goddess.

AURORA—*aka Eos—Greek*
Daughter of the Titans Hyperion and Theia. Sister of Helios and Selene. Mother of the winds Boreas, Zephyrus, Notus and Eurus. Also mother of Hesperus. Goddess of the dawn.

AYLEKETE—*dba Agbe—Fon, Africa*
A member of the Vodu family of gods. God of the sea.

AZI—*Buryat*
Red-haired earth spirits who seek human company. The witty Azi appreciate eloquence, musical talent, alcohol, tobacco and tea. They reward mortals who please them. Mortals who displease them forfeit their souls.

II

BAAL, BAB AND THE BASILISK

BAAL—*dba* Baal-zebub—*Canaan, Phoenicia and Ugarit*
God of storms, war, good harvests and fertility. Titles include Prince, Lord of Earth and Rider of the Clouds. He is the healing god and he resides upon the heights of Tsaphon.

BAAL HAMMON—*Carthage*
Husband of Tanit.

BAALAT—*Phoenicia*
The lady, queen of gods. She has a special fondness for books, libraries and writers. Her principal city is Byblos, which gave humans papyrus.

Papyrus was called byblos by the Greeks, who then applied the same word to books.

BAALSHAMIN—*Semite*
God of the sky.

BAB—*Egypt*
A somewhat disrespectful rogue of a god, but a good friend of Seth (*qv*) all the same.

BABA YAGA—*Slavonic*
The thunder witch who is the grandmother of the devil. She flies through the sky in an iron cauldron and sweeps away the traces of her passage with her broom. She is not to be trusted because she is cannibalistic.

BACCHUS—*dba* Dionysus and Liber—*Greek and Roman*
Son of Zeus and Semele, a mortal who was the daughter of King Cadmus of Thebes. God of wine, vegetation, fertility and the dramatic arts. During his festivals, slaves and prisoners are set free and the goods of debtors cannot be seized. Everybody's favorite—next to, possibly, Dionysus (*qv*).

BADB CATHA—*Celtic*
She is called the Battle Raven and her appearance bodes death.

BAIAME—*aka* Daramulun and Nurundere—*Australia*
Father of all things and master of life and death. He resides in a sky palace constructed of fresh water and quartz crystal.

BAJ BAJANIA—*Yakut (Siberia)*
The forest god beloved for his joyousness.

BALDER—*aka* Baldr—*German*

Son of Odin and Frigg. God of innocence, purity, beauty, justice and reconcilitation. Easily the wisest and kindest of the Aesir race of Gods. Balder is now in the custody of Hel, she who keeps the dead, after a slight problem involving some lethal mistletoe. At Ragnarok (*qv*), Balder will be released to create a new race of mortals who will be far less troublesome because these mortals will manage to live in justice and happiness.

BALI—*India*

Son of Prahlada. A demon who reigns over three worlds—akasa (heaven) where the sun shines but there are no clouds, apas (atmosphere) where clouds are found, and vasumdhara (earth) where mortals are generally found. He was so pure in his conduct that his bones became diamonds and his blood was changed to rubies.

BASILISK—*Africa and Switzerland*

A rather frightening-looking lizard that is able to run on water. Those who annoy it can be frozen in their tracks by its angry glare. It is generally found by those who are not looking for it. Areas to avoid are inaccessible regions of the Swiss Alps and African deserts.

BAST—*dba* Pasht—*Egypt*

Mother of Mahes. Goddess of life, fruitfulness and cats.

BAUCIS and PHILOMEN—*Greek*

An aged and impoverished mortal couple. They were residents of Phrygia who had nothing but their great devotion to each other. When Zeus and Hermes visited Phrygia disguised as mortals, no one would give them the time of day, much less a morsel to eat or a roof over their heads. Baucis and Philomen shared what little they had with the strangers. Zeus decided Phrygia was a mess, so he destroyed it by flood and saved only Baucis and Philomen. So that they would want for nothing, Zeus built them a temple and made them priests.

BEDA—*German*
A goddess.

BEFANA—*Italy*
An old woman who is as kind as she is ugly. Each January 5th she distributes sweets to good children and lumps of coal to bad ones.

BELATU-CADROS—*Gaul*
God of the destruction of enemies.

BELE—*aka* Tule, Azapane and Mba—*Sudan, Africa*
God of fear, mischief and trickery. He gave fire and water to humans.

BELENUS—*Celtic*
God in charge of the welfare of sheep and cattle. See BELTINE.

BELISAMA—*Gaul*
Goddess of the forge and of crafts.

BELLEROPHON—*Greek*
A foolish mortal who tried to ride Pegasus to Olympus. He fell off.

BELLONA—*Roman*
The goddess of war.

BELOGOB—*Slav*
God of the living.

BELTINE—*Celtic*
The feast of Belenus (*qv*). Generally celebrated the first of May.

BENDIS—*Thrace*
Goddess of the moon.

BENZAI-TEN—*dba* Benten and Benzai-tennyo—*Japan*
Goddess of eloquence, language, wisdom, knowledge, the arts, good fortune and water.

BEREGUINI—*aka* boginki—*Slav*
River nymphs. It is unfairly rumored that these nymphs steal newborn mortal children and leave behind their own deformed babies. This is a slanderous rumor. A river nymph would no more abandon her own child than would a mortal woman. Further, the incidence of children born with birth defects is no greater among river nymphs than it is among humans.

BES—*Egypt*
A dwarf god of great powers. God of music and dancing, protector of women in childbirth and protector against terrors.

BHIMA—*dba* Bhimsen and Bhimul Pen—*India*
Son of Vayu. God of rain. Noted for his heroic strength and courage.

BHUT—*India*
An evil spirit.

BIA—*Ashanti, Africa*
Elder son of Asase Ya and Nyame.

BINGO—*Bantu, Africa*

Son of Nzame and a mortal woman named Mboya. Teacher of mortals. When Bingo was thrown down from heaven by his jealous father, the great sorcerer Otoyum hid the manchild. Due to Otoyum's wise teachings, Bingo grew up to aid and teach the mortals.

BINZURU-SONJA—*Japan*

God of curing and fine vision. He is, himself, unable to escape pain; therefore, he helps all others to do so.

BISHAMON-TEN—*dba* Bishamontenno and Tamon-tennu—*Japan*

God of wealth, protector of human life and chaser of demons.

BITOL—*Maya*

Sky god, one of the seven gods who assisted in the creation of the world and its mortals.

BLACK MAGIC

Calling upon supernatural assistance to do harm to someone or something. Must be done with great exactitude. If any mistakes are made, or if the party called upon to render assistance does not wish to assist, the evil spell at once rebounds upon the spellcaster three-fold.

BOANN—*Celtic*

River goddess.

BOCHICA—*Chibcha Indian*

Supreme creator and lawgiver. Before he left the mortal plane, he imprinted the shape of his foot on a rock.

BONA DEA—*aka* Fauna and the Good Goddess—
   Roman
   Goddess of fertility. Her true name is not known
because she has refused to give one hint of it. She is a
great prophet, a dispenser of healing herbs and is
quite chaste. She also permits no wine to be imbibed
in her presence.

BOOK OF THE DEAD—*Egypt*
   A prayerbook placed in the coffin of deceased
Egyptians. Many of the prayers it contained were
those recited by the priests at the funeral. As such
prayers usually do, they wished the deceased peace,
happiness, joy and a speedy trip to the loving protection of heaven.

BOR—*German*
   Son of Buri. Husband of Bestla. Father of Odin,
Vili and Ve.

BOREAS—*Greek*
   Son of Astraeus and Eos. Father of two daughters, two sons and 12 mares which can race over the
ground without harming the grain. King of the
winds. In 480 B.C. the Athenians begged his assistance against the might of the Persian navy of Xerxes.
The Great Wind of the Wintery North blew his anger
at the Persian upstarts and 400 Persian ships sank
immediately.

BORVO—*dba* Bormo, Bormanus, Gramnnos, Belenos
   and Toutiorix—*Gaul*
   God of healing. God of hot springs.

BRAGI—*German*
   Husband of Idun. God of poetry. Chief poet of
the gods. God of skalds (poets).

BRAHMA—India

All that exists. The creator and the absolute. Other than that, he has four arms and four mouths.

BRANAB LLYR—*Celtic*

Son of Lyr. God of the sea, sailors, waves and storms. He is a fearless sailor who does not fear uncharted seas. He is the god of the dead and can restore humans to life. He is also a musician of some renown and his favorite instrument is the harp.

BRIAREUS—*Greek*

Son of Uranus and Gaea. Brother of Cottus and Gyes. The trio were known as the Hecatoncheires, or Hundred-Handed Ones. They were mighty giants, and Briareus had 50 heads. The brothers assisted Zeus in his contretemps with the Titans, but not without some soul-searching: The Titans were all blood relatives and their case was not without merit.

BRIGANTIA—*aka* Bridget or Brigit—*Celtic*

Daughter of Dagda. Goddess of the seasons, Goddess of doctors, poets and smiths. Goddess of women in childbirth.

BROWNIE—*Scotland and England*

A household spirit, quite small in size. They are fond of mortals and often attach themselves to a household to help with chores. They are nocturnal, mischievous and easily angered. They are also valiant and brave spirits who serve above and beyond their normal range of duties when the need arises. In times past, brownies have been known to ride horseback to fetch a midwife to attend at childbirth in weather no mortal would have dared go out in.

BRUT—*Greek and British*

At the direction of Diana, Brut the mortal and a group of Trojans founded Britain. At the time, the place was known as Albion and was inhabited by a race of giants.

BUNBULAMA—*Australia*

Goddess of rain.

BUGA—*Tungus*

The supreme god.

BUMBA—*Bakuba, Africa*

God of fire.

BUTO—*Egypt*

The god who guards Lower Egypt.

BUXENUS—*Gaul*

God of boxtrees. The boxtree is an evergreen, *Buxus sempervirens*, with small leaves and not very showy flowers. However, the wood of the tree is very hard and is extensively used for scientific instruments, quality furniture and musical instruments.

III

CALLIOPE, CALYPSO AND THE CYCLOPES TRIO

CABAGUIL—*Maya*

Known to his friends as Heart of the Sky. He is one of the seven gods who assisted in the creation of the world and of mortals.

CABALA—*aka* Kabala—*Jewish*

It means, quite simply, tradition. It refers to an attempt by Jewish mystics to understand the nature of God and the relationship between God and humans.

CALLIOPE—*Greek*

Daughter of Zeus and Mnemmosyne. Mother of Orpheus. The Muse of Eloquence and Poetry and thus the most distinguished of the nine Muses. Her name, incidentally, means beautiful voice. Mortals have bestowed this name upon a gaudily painted circus wagon with steam whistles which give out such piercing tones that they can be heard for a distance of ten miles. Most likely Calliope is not amused.

CALLISTO—*Greek*

Daughter of Lycaon, king of Arcadia. She was a nymph of the cult of Artemis, and vowed never to marry. She was raped by Zeus and bore him a son named Arcas. The whole thing upset Artemis, so naturally she took it out on Callisto by changing her into a bear.

CALYPSO—*Greek*

Daughter of Atlas. A sea nymph who lived on the island of Ogygia. She promised the human hero Odysseus immortality if he would live with her. He stayed for seven years but Zeus ordered Calypso to toss him out. She did, but supplied Odysseus with a raft and provisions for his journey.

CAMAXTLI—*Aztec*

God of war. Creator of fire. One of the four gods who created the world.

CAMAXTLI—*Maya*

God of fate.

CANDRA—*India*

God of the moon.

CAPRAKAN—*Maya*

Son of the giant Gukup Cakix and Chimalmat. Brother of Zipcna. God of earthquakes and mountains.

CASSANDRA—*Greek*

Daughter of Hecuba and Priam, king of Troy. Apollo fell in love with Cassandra and gave her the gift of prophecy. However, when Cassandra refused to hop into bed with Apollo, he flew into a snit and fixed it so that no one ever believed a word Cassandra said.

CASTOR and POLLUX—*Greek*

Twin sons of Zeus and Leda who were hatched from an egg. Protectors of sailors, they have been known to appear during storms as twin lights of St. Elmo's Fire. Although the lads are twins, Castor is mortal and Pollux is immortal. When Castor, who was a famous horse tamer at the time, was killed, Pollux was inconsolable. Now Zeus allows Castor and Pollux to take turns at life and death.

CECROPS—*Greek*

Half man and half snake. Founder of Athens, first king of Attica. Taught the inhabitants of the area to bury the dead, get married and read and write.

CENTAUR—*Greek*

The offspring of Ixion, the king of Lapithae (Thessaly), and a cloud. This last was not what Ixion intended. Actually, he had arranged a tryst with Hera, wife of Zeus. Zeus got wind of it, however, and fashioned a cloud into Hera's shape. Centaurs live chiefly around Mount Pelion in Thessaly, where some call them Ixionidae. They have the head, neck, arms and chest of a mortal and the body, legs and tail of a horse.

CENTZON TOTOCHTIN—*Aztec*

A drunken and immoral group of deities who meet frequently to enjoy themselves.

CERBERUS—*Greek*

Watchdog of Hades. He has three heads and the tail of a snake. If you are alive he won't let you in. If you are dead he won't let you out.

CERES—*Roman*

Daughter of Saturn and Rhea. Wife-sister of Jupiter. Mother of Proserpina. Goddess of grain, growing plants and the love that a mother bears for her child. Her festival is Ambarvalia, held in May.

CERUNNOS—*Celtic*

God of prosperity. His head is topped by a most attractive set of antlers.

CERKLICING—*Latvia*

God of fields and corn.

CESSAIR—*Celtic*

She is one of the greatest magicians ever to trod the soil of Earth. She was the first queen of Ireland and she inhabited the land after the Great Flood with her female followers.

CHAC MOL—*Maya*

God of thunder.

CHALCHIUHTLICUE—*Aztec*

Wife of Tlaloc. Goddess of the East. Ruler of the water sun Nahuiatl. Goddess of the sea, springs and all running water. Protectress of newborn babies and marriages.

CHANG-O—*aka* Heng-o—*China*
Wife of Yi. Goddess of the moon.

CHANGO—*Africa, South and Central America and the Caribbean*
Warrior god. Defends mortals against enemies who want their land, wealth and women.

CHAOS—*Greek*
The void which existed before the creation of the universe. Whether or not it contained the seeds of all life or was simply empty is a matter of speculation similar to the continuing speculation as to whether or not the universe is expanding, contracting or staying in the same shape it was always in before. However, it is known that Uranus and Gaea arose from Chaos and gave birth to the Titans. That is more than is known for certain about any of those other theories.

CHARON—*Greek*
Son of Erebus and Nyx. Employed as a ferryman to conduct the dead across the River Acheron, one of the messier of the five rivers of Hades. Charon's fee is a piece of money previously placed under the tongue of the deceased. Living persons who want to go to Hades need a golden bough obtained from the Cumaean Sibyl.

CHEBELDEI—*Siberia*
Inhabitants of the lower world. They are composed mainly of iron and are black in color. They do not particularly care for human beings.

CHEMOSH—*Moabite*
National god of the Moabites. A jack-of-all-trades and a master of most.

CHERUB—*Mesopotamia*

Guardians of important places. They intercede with the divinities and for the divinities. They are winged figures with human heads and animal bodies, and closely resemble sphinxes.

CH'I-YOU—*China*

God of war, weapons, smiths and dancers. He has sharp pointed horns, an iron head and a brow of bronze. His hair bristles like spears. He eats stone, iron and sand and is otherwise fearsome in appearance and behavior. However, he does love to dance.

CHICKCHARNEY—*Andros Island, Bahamas*

A small feathered and furred spirit of the forest.

CHICOMECOATL—*Aztec*

Goddess of maize (corn).

CHIE—*Chibcha Indian*

A fun-loving goddess who told mortals that merrymaking, joy and laughter should supplant the rule of law. This severely annoyed Bochica, god of law, who turned her into an owl.

CHIMERA—*Greek*

Daughter of Typhon and Echidna. Born in a volcano. Due to the circumstances of her birth, Chimera had a foul temper. She was as beautiful as the daughter of a father with 100 serpent heads and a mother who was half female and half serpent could be expected to be. Chimera had the hindquarters of a dragon, the midsection of a goat and the forequarters of a lion. Pegasus and Bellerophon slew her, which was perhaps for the best.

CHIMINAGUA—*Chibcha Indian, Colombia*

The omnipotent master who created the earth. His method of doing so was to enclose the light, become bright, rise and free the light. So simple a child could do it.

CHIRAKAN—IXMUCANE—*Maya*

The goddess who was brought forth when four of the gods who created the world split themselves and became four additional beings.

CHIRON—*Greek*

Son of Kronus and Philyra, one of the Oceanids. Chiron was born a centaur because Cronus had changed himself into a stallion and Philyra into a mare so his wife Rhea would be deceived. Rhea was not deceived one bit and Philyra realized that about nine months later. Chiron was educated by Apollo and Artemis and studied medicine, music, hunting and prophecy. He was a brilliant educator and became the teacher of such notable mortals as Herakles, Jason, Achilles and Asclepius. However, any contact with Herakles was bound to bring disaster. Herakles got into a brawl and shot Chiron with a poisoned arrow. Chiron, who was immortal, suffered such grave pain from his wound that he gave his immortality to Prometheus and died.

CHLORIS—*Greek*

Wife of Zephyrus. Goddess of places shaded by trees, shrubs and vines. Several notable Greek mortal females bore her name. It did not bring them any luck.

CHOLMUS—*Siberia*

Creator of animals.

CHONSU—*Egypt*
God of the moon.

CIHUATETO—*Aztec*
Spirits who accompany the sun. These are women who die in childbirth and are rewarded with the gift of eternal life.

CIRCE—*Greek*
Daughter of Helios and Perse. A sorceress who lives on the island of Aeaea. She gave shelter to the mortal Odysseus and his crew after the Trojan War, but the table manners of Odysseus' crew were so abominable that Circe turned them into swine.

CLIO—*Greek*
Daughter of Zeus and Mnemosyne. The Muse of History.

COATLICUE—*Aztec*
Mother goddess. Mother of the god of war Huitzilopochtli. Can transform herself into a ravishing beauty, given the need for such a thing.

COMUS—*Greek (adopted by the Romans)*
Son of Bacchus and Circe. God of revelry, drunkeness and mirth. He is in charge of entertaining the gods and presides over all decently organized festive occasions. He is a winged god who is normally clad in white and has a youthful appearance.

CONCORDIA—*Roman*
Goddess of peace and harmony.

CONSUS—*Roman*
One of the earth gods. The keeper of stored agricultural crops. On his feast days, farm and dray

horses were not permitted to work and attended the festivities.

CORYBANT—*Greek*

The first human forms on earth. Thus, simply everyone claims parenthood, including Apollo, Rhea and Thalia. In any case, the hectic and abandoned dances they perform have the power to cure mental illness.

COYOLXAUHQUI—*Aztec*

Daughter of Coatlicue. Sister of the war god Huitzilopochtli. He dismembered her during a power struggle and she has not been the same since.

COYOTE—*Crow Indian, North America*

The god who created the earth and all living creatures. Coyote built a boat in which he drifted while the earth was covered with water. He then told two ducks to dive and bring back mud. One duck did not return, but the duck that did had the required mud. From this mud, Coyote created the earth and its creatures.

CRINISUS—*Greek*

One of the river gods.

CRNOBOG—*dba* Crnoglav—*Slav*

The black god of the dead.

CRONUS—*aka* Kronos, Kronus, Chronos and Chronus—*Greek*

Son of Uranus and Gaea. Brother of Oceanus, Coeus, Crius, Iapetus, Hyperion, Rhea, Theia, Tethys, Phoebe, Themis and Mnemosyne. Brother-husband of Rhea. Father of Zeus, Hestia, Demeter,

Hera, Hades and Poseidon. youngest of the 12 Titans.
God of fate. God of agriculture. Became king of the
Titans for a short period after castrating his father. For
this, mortals claim he is a great civilizer.

CU CHULAIN—*aka* Setanta, Cuchulainn and the
   Watchdog of Chulain—*Celtic*
   Son of Lug the sun god and the mortal woman
Dechtire who was the wife of the prophet Sualtim and
the sister of King Conchobar of Ulster. God of heat
and light. Immune to most magic spells. Himself
taught magic by witch Scatbach, Queen of Darkness.
Known throughout Ireland as a fearless warrior and
great lover.

CUPID—*Roman*
   Emerged from a silver egg and is bisexual. He
has golden wings, four heads and is responsible for
setting the world in motion. Stories that he is the son
of Venus are myth; Cupid does not resemble Venus in
the slightest. They get on quite well together, though,
because, at Cupid's whim, mortals fall irrevocably in
love. He is also susceptible to bribes.

CYBELE—*Asia*
   The great mother goddess. Goddess of fertility
and nature. Founder of cities. The guardian of
civilization.

CYCLOPES—*Greek*
   Sons of Uranus and Gaea. They are Brontes,
Steropes and Arges. They manufactured thunderbolts for Zeus, Poseidon's trident and Hades's helmet
of invisibility. They are also responsible for the building of many of the massive and ancient constructions
of stone that mortals find around the world. The

Cyclopes are currently employed as assistants of Hephaestus, blacksmith to the gods, in Mount Etna.

CYRENE—*Greek*

Daughter of the naiad Creusa and the mortal Hypseus, king of the Lapiths. Apollo fell madly in love with her and took her to Africa, where he built her a city.

IV

DAIKOKU AND THE DANSE MACABRE

DABOG—*aka* Vid, Daba and Hromi (Lame) Daba—*Slav*
 Supreme God. God of the sun. God of the herd.
God of precious metals.

DAEDALUS—*Greek*
 A mortal inventor, artist and architect. Among
his most lasting inventions are the plumb line, car-
pentry, the axe and the awl. Alas, his vanity was
uncontrollable and his downfall as well. When his
nephew Talos proved to be more skilled and talented,
Daedalus killed him and fled to Crete. There he

became involved with the notorious King Minos and built the labyrinth for the Minotaur.

DAEMONES—*Greek*

A family of affectionate and benevolent elementals who inhabit fields, forests, deserts, mountains, lakes, valleys, streams, oceans and towns. They live, love and suffer in much the same manner as mortals do, but they are immortal. Because they cannot die, they have been the targets of slander and libel from jealous and bigoted humans who label them evil demons.

DAEVAS—*aka* Devas and Devs—*Persia*

Malevolent spirits.

DAGDA—*dba* Dagde, Dagodevas, Eochaid Ollathair and Ruad Ro-fhessa—*Celtic*

Omnipotent god of complete knowledge. Master of life and death. Dispenser of plenty. A warrior, magician and artisan. He summons the seasons by playing his harp, and his cauldron can supply food for the entire world.

DAGON—*Mesopotamia*

God of vegetation. Half man and half fish.

DAIKOKU—*dba* Daikoko-tenn and the Great Black One—*Japan*

God of wealth and happiness. Protector of the soil. Can make wishes of mortals come true. Creates gold with the aid of his magic mallet.

DAIMON—*Greek*

An individual member of the daemones family.

DAN—*aka* Dan Ayido Hwedo—*Fon, Africa*

Son of the twins Lisa and Mahu. God of unity and life.

DANA—*aka* Donu and Don—*Celtic*

Wife of Beli. The mortal Celtic race is descended from Dana. Her people are the Tuatha De Danaan who came to Ireland many centuries ago from the Isles of the West and returned there later on. Some, who could not bear to leave the land they called Erinn, took the name Aes sidhe and remained. They dwell beneath the surface of the land and vanish and reappear at will. In a just battle, they will fight beside mortals. When they fight, they go armed with lances of blue flame and shields of pure white.

DANAUS—*Greek*

Grandson of Poseidon. Twin brother of Aegyptus. Father of 50 daughters known as the Danaids. When a problem surfaced concerning the inheritance of Danaus and Aegyptus, the latter, who had 50 sons, suggested that they all marry the daughters of Danaus—thus solving the problem. Danaus didn't like the idea and resisted, but the marriage took place anyway. Danaus was most unhappy and ordered all his daughters to kill their husbands on their collective wedding night. All obeyed save Hypermnestra, who would not slay her husband Lynceus. Lynceus then killed Danaus and solved the inheritance problem.

DANSE MACABRE—*aka* The Dance of Death

During the Middle Ages, European mortals believed that the dead had nothing better to do but get up at night and dance all over their graves. Any person foolish enough to be enticed into dancing with a skeleton was in danger of death. Any skeleton foolish enough to get up and dance with a mortal was in danger of falling to pieces, but most mortals never considered this.

DAPHNE—*Greek*

Daughter of the River Peneius. She is a mountain nymph and a priestess of Mother Earth. She is beloved of the mortal Leucippus (since deceased) and the god Apollo. Daphne, unfortunately, is unable to love anyone. Cupid, in a fit of spite, shot her with a lead arrow and she has not yet recovered.

DARDANUS—*Greek*

Son of Zeus and Electra, daughter of Atlas. He sailed from Samothrace to Troas in a raft made of hides and founded the city of Dardania.

DARZAMAT—*Latvia*

Goddess of gardens.

DAZBOG—*Slav*

God of wealth.

DEAE MATRES—*Celtic*

The trinity of mother goddesses who rule fertility and creativity.

DEIVAI—*Prussian*

A respectful term which means goddess.

DELKA—*Latvia*

Goddess of newborn children.

DEMETER—*Greek*

Daughter of Cronus and Rhea. Wife of Poseidon. Mother of Persephone, by Zeus. The nature goddess who rules the fruitfulness of the earth. When Persephone was abducted by Hades, Demeter created winter.

DENG—*Dinka, Africa*

Son of the goddess Abuk. God of rain.

DERCETO—*Greek*

Goddess of fertility. She is a quite beautiful woman with the tail of a fish.

DEUCALION—*Greek*

Son of Prometheus. When Zeus punished mortals for their lack of respect by flooding the earth, Deucalion and his wife Pyrrah were the sole survivors.

DEVING ISCHING—*Latvia*

God of horses.

DIANA—*Roman*

Mother and protectress of wildlife. Goddess of the hunt. Goddess of young maidens and travellers.

DIANCECHT—*Celtic*

Father of Miach. God of healing and health who restores humans to life. When King Nuada of the Tuatha De Danaann lost his right hand in battle, Diancecht replaced it with an articulated one made of silver. Miach then replaced that hand with Nuada's own hand. Diancecht slew Miach. Some claimed it was jealousy. Diancecht said it was the disrespectful manner in which the replacement was done.

DIDO—*aka* Elissa—*Greek*

Daughter of Belus, king of Tyre. Sister of Pygmalion. When Pygmalion became king, he killed Elissa's husband Acerbas because he wanted his money. Elissa escaped to Libya where she founded the city of Carthage, became its queen and took the name Dido. It is rumored that she killed herself with a knife when Aeneas abandoned her. Thus came the expression "cutting a Dido," to denote a frivolous and showy act. However, it is extremely doubtful that Dido slew herself over the loss of a single male.

DIKE—*Greek*

Daughter of Temis the Titan. Goddess of justice.

DINOSAUR—*Modern*

The name currently applied to the dragon family.

DIONYSUS—*Greek*

Son of Zeus and Semele. God of fertility, wine and vegetation. His followers are the Satyrs, Sileni and the Bacchantes. Mortals who disobey Dionysus are struck mad.

DIS PATER—*Gaul*

The father of the race of Gauls. His wife is the Goddess-Without-Name who gave birth to all plants, animals and mortals.

DIVIRIKS—*Lithuania*

Deity of the rainbow.

DJANGGAWULS—*Australia*

The sisters Miralaidj and Bildjiwuraroju, who are daughters of the sun goddess. They are goddesses of fertility who created human beings and vegetation.

DOH—*Yenisei (Siberia)*

One of the greatest magicians. While traveling, Doh would fly over the waves until he became weary. Then he would create islands to rest on.

DOHIT—*Mosetene Indian*

The god who created the first mortal from clay.

DOLA—*Slav*

The spirit of mortal fate.

DOMFE—*Kurumba, Africa*

The water god, god of rain and wind. He gave the first food-bearing seeds to humans.

DONGO—*Songhoi, Africa*
God of thunder.

DORIS—*Greek*
Wife of Nereus (*qv*). Mother of Thetis, a sea nymph. Grandmother of Achilles.

DRAGONS
The race of warm-blooded creatures, often winged and with long tails. Dragons are scaled and range in color from golden, through emerald and ruby, to pure white. Dragons can spit fire when angered, but are generally benevolent, friendly and intellectual. The species is quite large, but these elusive and shy creatures are well capable of successfully concealing themselves from mortal eyes. Scientists of the mortal persuasion have attempted to reconstruct dragon bones and have brought forth many theories about them. The dragons are still laughing.

DRUIDS—*Celtic*
A religious order open to both male and female humans. Druids do a consistently good job of sustaining the powers of prosperity of the land. Those lands which have abandoned Druids have never quite recovered from such foolishness. Druid functions include arbitration, pronouncements on public policy, enchantment and divination. Some Druids, such as Merlin, are expert in shape-changing. Others, such as the prophetess Veleda, are seers. Druid bards, or bardoi, specialize in the composition of songs and tales which transmit history and knowledge. Druids do not use writing. It is not necessary for a Druid to write anything down in order to remember it.

DRYADS—*aka* Hamadryads—*Greek*

Nymphs of the trees and woods. Oak trees are sacred to dryads and a dryad will die in the defense of her tree. This is not an environmental hang-up. When a dryad's tree dies, so does she.

DUALISM

The theory that the world is composed of two basically different things—light and dark, good and evil, male and female, etc. This is a perceptual problem and influences reality only as much as it is permitted to do.

DWARF—*Not to be confused with short mortals*

These supernatural beings are widespread members of the fairy folk. The Fon of Dahomey know them as azizan, or little people of the forest. The Ashanti of Ghana call them mmoetia, or forest dwarves. Europeans call them leprechauns, trolls, gnomes, etc. The metal work done by dwarves is universally superb because their sharp eyesight permits them to obtain a fine detail work mortals cannot duplicate without technological assistance.

DWYN—*dba* Dwynwen—*Celtic*

God of love.

DYAUSH—*India*

The first supreme god.

V

ELIXIRS, ELVES AND EROS

EA—*Babylon*
Father of Marduk. God of the deep sea. God of wisdom. He, Anu and Enlil rule the cosmos, with Ea reserving the right to rule all waters surrounding the earth. He is the patron of magicians, healers, and all who practice the arts and crafts properly.

EBISU—*Japan*
God of fishermen.

EC—*Yenisei (Siberia)*
Husband of Khosadam. High god.

ECHO—*Greek*

A mountain nymph who was a servent of Hera. Hera claimed that Echo talked entirely too much, so she deprived the unfortunate child of her speech, permitting her only to repeat the last syllable of every word she heard. Hera smugly claimed that this would teach Echo not to be such a chatterbox. Instead, Echo pined away until nothing but her voice was left.

EHECATL—*Aztec*

God of the wind. He begins the movement of the sun and sweeps the high roadways of the rain god with his breath.

EL—*Ugarit*

Husband of Athirat, father of Shahar and Shalim. Supreme god and creator. Father of gods, mortals, and time. He is a wise, kind and merciful god and is ancient beyond human understanding. He presently dwells quite peacefully in the hollow of the Abyss at the Source of All Rivers.

ELECTRA—*Greek*

There are two goddesses who bear this name. Electra, daughter of Oceanus and wife of Thaumas, is the mother of Iris, goddess of the rainbow, and of the Harpies. Electra, the daughter of Atlas, spent some time with Zeus and then gave birth to Dardanus, ancestor of the Trojan kings.

ELEMENTAL

Essentially a primal being which is close kin to any, or all, of the four elements—earth, air, fire and water. Elementals are quite independent types.

ELLER-KONGE—*dba* Erlkonig and Erlking—*German*

A rather nasty goblin who hangs around the Black Forest and lures men and children to their death with false promises and visions.

ELIXIR

Any ancient medical drug which modern physicians do not understand, cannot duplicate and generally deride.

ELVES—*Europe*

Smaller in size than the average dwarf. Members of the fairy folk. Elves range in size from two to three inches in height. They are extremely delicate in appearance but have an incredible strength which allows them to hurl huge boulders great distances and shake the walls of the homes of mortals. Elves hibernate in the winter, but are usually awake by the first day of spring. They are naturally invisible to all humans except those born on a Sunday, but any given elf can become visible at will. Few do. They are sensitive and easily offended, thus they have few dealings with other parties.

ELYSIUM—*Greek*

Heaven.

EMMA-O—*Japan*

God of the dead, Master of Hell and he who punishes sinners. He has the power to prolong life and to resurrect the dead.

ENCELADUS—*Greek*

Son of Tartarus and Gaea. He was one of the hundred-handed Titans who made war against the Olympian Gods. He was slain with a thunderbolt and buried under Mount Etna. This explains the mountain's subsequent eruptions.

ENDYMION—*Greek*

A mortal who has been sleeping for centuries on Mount Latmus in Asia Minor. A moon goddess named Selene saw him sleeping there quite normally many years ago. She fell in love with his beauty and has resolved never to let him awaken to age and eventually die. She visits him nightly and, so far, she has borne him 50 daughters.

ENERGUMEN—*aka* daimonizomenos or welfare recipients

Mortals believed energumen were under the dominion of evil spirits and this was the reason everything went wrong for them. In third century Europe, there were so many energumen that churches kept records of them. They received free lodging, clothing, food and pretty much of anything else they wanted. All this support was courtesy of the alms of the faithful.

ENKI—*Sumer*

Son of Enlil and Nammu. Lord of Earth. God of the air.

EOSTRE—*Anglo-Saxon*

Goddess of the Spring. Protectress of fertility, goddess of rebirth and friend to all children. To amuse the children, Eostre changed her beautiful pet bird into a rabbit. The rabbit further delighted the children by bringing forth brightly colored eggs, which Eostre gave the children as gifts.

EPHIALTES—*Greek*

Son of Poseidon, twin brother of Otus. These two giants were called the Aloadae. Quite inventive sorts, they once piled Mount Ossa on Mount Pelion in an attempt to reach Heaven and attack the gods.

EPIMETHEUS—*Greek*

Son of Iapetus and Clymene. Brother of Prometheus. Zeus, who was a bit put out with mortals at the time, created Pandora to punish men and gave her to Epimetheus as a wife. Zeus gave her a lovely box for her dowry and told her the gifts inside would be truly amazing. As Zeus planned, the curious Pandora opened the box only to find inside sorrows, ills and diseases which her brother-in-law Prometheus had locked up so they could not trouble humans. Of course, Pandora took the rap for the whole thing. See PANDORA.

EPONA—*Celtic*

Goddess of horses, mules and cavalrymen. She protects, feeds and shelters them. Roman soldiers who learned of her quickly became converts and spread her worship wherever they went.

ERATO—*Greek*

One of the nine Muses. She is the muse of lyric and love poems and, when she feels like it, of mimicry.

ERDA—*German*

The anciently wise earth goddess.

EREBUS—*Greek*

Son of Chaos. He dwells in a rundown section of Hades.

ERIS—*Greek*

Goddess of strife and discord.

ERISHKIGAL—*Sumer*

Goddess of the land of no return.

ERLIK—*Samoyed*

God of the netherworld. A bit of a bumbler who once accidentally handed the sun and moon to the devil. He has also stated publicly that human beings really should graze like cattle.

EROS—*Greek*

Son of Aphrodite and either Zeus or Ares or Mercury. (Aphrodite really is terrible at keeping track of things like this.) God of love, power and sexual prowess. He does not age, but youthens. Husband of the mortal Psyche. Eros is often confused with Cupid by mortals who don't know any better.

ESCHETEWUARHA—*Chamacoco Indian*

Wife of the Great Spirit. Ruler of the world. Mother of the rain.

ESCHU—*aka* Legba—*Yoruba, Africa*

The deities who serve as messengers between gods and mortals. They are indispensable but nasty.

ESEGE—*Buryat*

The god who rules the western sky.

ESHMUN—*Sidon (Phoenicia)*

God of the city.

ESUS—*Gaul*

God of woodcutters. He prunes the tree of life with cruel cuts so that it will flower, bear fruit and find strength.

EUANDROS—*dba* Evander—*Greek*

Son of Hermes and the river nymph Themis. Although born in Greece, he left there and settled in Italy on the bank of the Tiber River, where he was welcomed to the neighborhood by the Roman god Faunus. Euandros introduced laws, writing and other arts and skills.

EUMOLPUS—*Greek*
Son of Poseidon and Chione, the daughter of Boreas. He was the founder of the Eleusinian Mysteries.

EUPHROSYNE—*Greek*
One of the three Graces. She is joy.

EUROPA—*Phoenicia*
A mortal princess. Daughter of Agenor and sister of Cadmus. Zeus, as he so often did, fell in love and decided he must have Europa. He changed himself into a white bull and, while she was bathing at the seashore, he lured her onto his back and swam off to Crete. Europa bore Zeus three sons—Minos, Rhadamanthus and Sarpedon. In return, Zeus gave her a man of bronze named Talos whose mission was to guard Crete. Europa was also given a spear that never missed its mark and a dog that always found her prey. Europa later married Asterius, king of Crete. When she died, Zeus made her a fertility goddess.

EURYDICE—*Greek*
A mountain valley nymph. Wife of Orpheus. She died soon after marriage, and Orpheus, who loved her deeply, journeyed to Hades to win her release. He sang and played upon his lyre until the lords of Hades wept at such love and grief. They gave Eurydice permission to leave but sternly warned Orpheus not to look back to see if she was behind him. He did and she was taken from him forever.

EUTERPE—*Greek*

One of the nine Muses. She claims to have invented the flute. Terpsichore also claims to have invented the flute and she has asked Euterpe to be content with inventing the tragic chorus. As of now, the quarrel is still unresolved.

EVADNE—*Greek*

Daughter of Poseidon and Pitane. Mother of the boychild Iamus by Apollo. Iamus is the ancestor of the prophetic Iamidae clan of Olympia.

VI

FAITH AND FRAVARTIN

FAFNIR—*German*

Son of the Magician Hreidmar. He guards the gold which was paid as a death-price for Otr, his brother. Otr was killed by Loki while Otr was fishing. The best that can be said in Loki's defense is that it was accidental. Otr had taken the shape of an otter and Loki did not know that the otter he killed was Otr.

FAGUS—*Gaul*

God of beech trees.

FAIRIES—*aka* Fairy Folk, Fata, Fatae, etc.

These minor gods and deities include ogres, goblins, hobgoblins, fées, nymphs, mermaids, fadas, some witches, trolls, brownies, leprechauns and, oddly enough, dragons. They are a numerous people who inhabit all parts of the earth and several nearby moons and planets. They are capable of great works of enchantment and magic.

FAITH

The moving factor in the existence of the gods, whether they like to admit it or not. The power of any god or goddess is directly drawn from the force of belief of worshippers. As belief wanes, so does power. As power wanes, so does belief. There isn't much that can be done about it.

FAMILIAR

The pet of a witch or wizard. You cannot, as some misbegotten mortals believe, do physical harm to a witch or a wizard by injuring one of their pets. What is accomplished is that the witch or wizard becomes very, very angry.

FAND—*Celtic*

Wife of Manannan, god of the sea.

FATA MORGANA

An enchantress who dwells beneath the water. She can raise castles on the surface of the water which are probably better than the ones mortals build on sand.

THE FATES—*Greek and Roman*

Daughters of Moira, who assigns each mortal her or his own destiny. The fates are: Clotho, she who spins the thread of life; Lachesis, she who measures it; and Atropos, she who severs it.

FAUNA—*aka* Marica—*Roman*
Wife of Faunus.

FAUNUS—*Roman*
Son of Picus. God of fields, shepherds and prophecy. Leader of the fauns, the Roman branch of the Greek satyrs. Fauns and/or satyrs resemble humans somewhat except for the fact that they have short horns, pointed ears, tails and goat's feet.

FEBRUUS—*Roman*
God of purification who dwells in the underworld.

FENRIR—*German*
The giant wolf, sworn enemy of the gods.

FERONIA—*ROMAN*
The deity who protects freedmen.

FETISH
A lucky charm, unless you're a psychologist.

FLOOD, The Great—*dba* The Deluge
When Atlantis was destroyed in the process of continental drift, the inrush of waters created by the original rift created a monstrous wave which destroyed civilization. Only those who had been warned by geologists that a massive upheaval in the crust of the planet was imminent escaped. Since most centers of civilization were located in coastal or riverbank areas, the destruction was almost complete as far as civilized mortals were concerned. Hence, the impression has persisted that the entire surface of the planet was covered by water. Such was not the case.

FLORA—*Roman*
Goddess of flowers and springtime.

FOMORS—*Celtic*
A race of giants.

FORTUNETELLING

Attempts by mortals to predict the future without the aid of the gods. This takes such forms as chartomancy, cleromancy, sortilege, palomancy, crystallomancy, hydromancy, lithomancy, oneiromancy, scyphomancy, aeromancy, alectryomancy, cledonism, oomancy, and rhabdomancy. Those are only a few of the many forms. Mortal fortunetelling is an interesting example of the form of an art taking precedence over the control of an art. Watching a human try to tell a fortune is equal to listening to a tone deaf person trying to sing opera.

FORTUNA—*Roman*

Goddess of women, fortune and fertility.

FRAVARTIN—*Persia*

Singular of the plural, Fravashi. She-Who-Is-Many is Fravashi. Fravashi is composed of the souls of all living creatures, including the Not-Yet-Born. She is the defender of all living creatures.

FREY—*aka* Freyr and Fricco—*German*

Son of Njord, god of the sea and of peace and prosperity. Brother of Freyja, goddess of love and beauty. Frey is the god of sun and rain .and of fruitfulness.

FREYA—*aka* FREYJA—*German*

Daughter of Njord. Sister of Frey. Leader of the Valkeyries. Not to be confused with Frigg or Frigga, wife of Odin. Odin does not get them confused and no one else should either. Freya is the goddess of love and beauty and endless rebirth. She dispenses wealth if you deserve it, and guarantees oaths. She receives half of the warriors slain in battle. They go to her palace, Sessrymnir, which is located in Folkvang. The other warriors are received in Valhalla by Odin.

FRIGG—*aka* Frigga—*German*

Wife of Odin. Mother of Balder and Hoth. Goddess of the sky. Frigg knows the future of humankind, but she will not reveal it to anyone.

FROST GIANTS—*aka* Ice Giants—*German*

Foes of the gods. This race arose from the sweat of the first giant, Ymir. They are human in form, but their powers are godlike.

FU-HSI—*China*

The god of vegetation and the inventor of writing.

FUDO-MYOO—*Japan*

The god who protects against calamities, great dangers and fire and theft. He is fond of mortals and gives them his complete support in all their enterprises.

FUKUROKUJU—*Japan*

The star god. He is easily recognizable because the length of his head is nearly equal to the length of his body.

FURIES—*dba* Erinyes (The Raging Ones)—*Greek*

They are: Allecto the Unceasing, Megaera the Grudging and Tisiphone the Avenging. They make their homes in Tartarus, the penal section of Hades, and work independently of the gods of Olympus. The furies punish such foul crimes as ingratitude, inhospitality, disrespect, harshness, perjury and homicide. They are not particularly vindictive. In fact, they are impartial and impersonal. They will simply pursue a wrongdoer until he is driven mad and dies. Then they will continue to punish that wrongdoer after death.

FYLGIA—plural FYLGJIR—*German*

Either the corporeal shadow of a sleeping person which acts of its own volition or a demonic ghost. It all depends a lot on who is trying to plead innocent to what.

VII

GAD TO GYGES

GAD—*Canaan*
God of fortune.

GAEA—*dba* Gaia and Ge—*Greek*
First-born of Chaos. Mother of the Titans, cyclopes, furies, giants and tree nymphs. Also mother of Pontos and Uranus. Goddess of the earth, goddess of marriage and goddess of death and what lies thereafter.

GALATEA—*Greek*
A sea nymph. The well-known cyclops Polyphemus was in love with her. She rejected him in

favor of a mortal shepherd named Acis. When Polyphemus discovered them *in flagrante delicto*, he lost what little temper he normally had and dropped a rock on Acis. Poor Acis went to pieces. Galatea fled into the sea. Acis was transformed into a river and he joined her. Polyphemus was not amused—but then he never was.

GAMAB—*aka* Ganna, Gawa, Gaunab—*Damaras, Africa*
Supreme God and creator of the world. He lives beyond the stars and chooses mortals who shall follow him through the abyss to the stars. Male mortals who do so are called Gamagu. Females are called Gamati.

GANYMEDE—*Greek*
A mortal, son of Tros and Callirhos. Zeus hired him on as cupbearer to the gods of Mount Olympus to replace Hebe. This annoyed several other individuals who then began circulating rumors that Zeus and Ganymede had a thing going between them.

GARUDA—*India*
The godbird who carries Vishnu.

GEB—*Egypt*
Son of Shu and Tefnut. Brother-husband of Nut. Father of Osiris, Isis, Seth and Nephthys. God of Earth.

GEFION—*German*
Goddess of fertility and virginity. She mothered a hardy breed. Her sons, disguised as oxen and hitched to a plow, tore the island of Seeland (Denmark) from the soil of Sweden and left behind Lake Malar.

GEUSH URVAN—*Persia*
An assistant to the Amesha Spenta Vohu Manab.

GHOST
The soul of a dead person.

GINNUNGAGAP—*German*
A rather large chasm in which the universe was created during a spontaneous union of heat and cold.

GIRRU—*Sumer*
God of fire. God of light. Patron of civilization. Messenger of the gods.

GLAUCUS—*Greek*
A sea god who uttered prophecies.

GLETI—*Dahomey*
Goddess of the moon.

GNOMES—*Europe*
Fairy folk who live in the earth and mine precious minerals. They have always been kindly disposed toward mortal miners.

GOBANNON—*Celtic*
God of blacksmiths.

GOIBNIU—*aka* Govannon—*Celtic*
Son of Dana and Bel. God of forges. A brewmaster so supreme that his beer gave the drinker immortality.

GOR—*Africa*
God of thunder.

GORGONS—*Greek*
They are Stheno, Euryale and the infamous Medusa. They dwell in Hades and are not particularly lovable. Their bodies are covered with impenetrable scales, their hands are made of brass, they have tusks instead of teeth and their hair is full of snakes. They are immortal and their gaze can turn mortals to stone.

When Perseus cut off Medusa's head, it was believed that she died. She did not, and the entire incident has done nothing to improve her nasty disposition.

THE GRACES—*Greek*

Daughters of Zeus. They are Aglaia the Brilliant, Euphrosyne the Joyful and Thalia the Flowering. They love all things beautiful and bestow talent upon mortals.

GRYPHON—*dba* Griffon or Griffin—*Scythia*

These strong and vigilant beasts have the head of an eagle, the body of a lion and enormous wings. They destroy those who try to steal.

GUKUMATZ—*Maya*

God of the sky. One of the seven gods who assisted in the creation of the world and of mortals.

GUKUP CAKIX—*Maya*

Husband of Chimalmat. Father of Zipacna and Caprakan. A rather stupid giant who pretended to be the sun and the moon. He came to a bad end.

GUN—*Fon, Africa*

Son of Mahu and Lisa. Twin of Xevioso. God of iron. God of war.

GWYDION—*Celtic*

God of civilization. An eloquent magician who loved the arts but could also battle well when the need arose.

GYGES—*aka* Gugu—*Lydia*

A mortal shepherd who found an enchanted ring on the body of a strange man discovered inside a brazen horse. The ring made the wearer invisible. With the aid of the ring, Gyges became king of Lydia.

VIII

HACHA'KYUM, THE GOD OF REAL PEOPLE

HACHA'KYUM—*Lacandon Maya*
    The god of real people. If you are not a Lacandon Maya, you are not a real person.

HACHIMAN—*Japan*
    God of war.

HADAD—*Semite*
    God of thunderstorms.

HADES—*Greek*
    God of the netherworld.

HALL OF ODIN—*Scandinavian*

Not a building. These are the rocks from which the mortals called Beserkers jump into the sea when they are tired of living.

HAMADRYADS—*Greek*

Tree nymphs.

HAN—*China*

The main river of the sky. Humans call it the Milky Way. It is more properly known as Silver Han, Han of the Stars or Han of the Sky.

HANUMAN—*India*

The monkey god. He is an extremely virile deity even though he is completely chaste.

HARMONIA—*Greek*

Daughter of Areas and Aphrodite. Wife of Cadmus, founder of Thebes. Hephaestus made a necklace for Harmonia that conferred irresistible beauty upon the wearer but it also brought ill-luck to anyone but Harmonia. This caused problems after Harmonia's death.

HARMONY OF THE SPHERES

All planets in their orbits send out musical tones caused by their motions. Each solar system has its own peculiar melody and thus can be recognized sight unseen.

HARPIES—*Greek*

Goddesses of storms. Principal among them are Podarge the Swiftfooted, Aello the Stormswift, Ocepete the Swiftwing and Celaeno the Dark. They have been depicted as hideous beasts by mortals who are afraid of thunder and lightning. Actually, they are winged women of an ethereal beauty.

HARUSPICES—*Etruria*

An individual haruspex foretells events by interpreting abnormal meteorological events, unusual growths and births of deformed humans and animals. At least that was the belief of the benighted Romans who made a practice of importing them to advise rulers. Actually, the haruspices told the rulers of Etruria what the weather was going to be like for their picnics.

HATHOR—*Egypt*

Goddess of love, mirth and joy. Goddess of the sky. Protects infants and consoles the dead.

HECATE—*Greek*

A Titan. Daughter of Perses. Goddess of abundance and eloquence. Goddess of the night. She is honored in the heavens, the earth and the seas as one who bestows or withholds pleasure, victory and wealth. She is the only Titan that Zeus has permitted to remain in power.

HEH—*Egypt*

God of the immeasurable. See ISLAND OF FLAME for further reference.

HEHET—*Egypt*

Goddess of the immeasurable. See above.

HEIMDALL—*German*

Son of Odin and the nine virgin daughters of Geirrendour the Giant. That is to say, all nine daughters stuck together and Geirrendour never was able to figure out which one of them was no longer a virgin. God of light and Guardian of the Bifrost Bridge, which connects Midgard with Asgard. His castle Himinbiorg is at the highest point of the bridge.

Heimdall can see great distances day and night and his hearing is so acute that he can hear the grass grow. This makes him an excellent guardian. He will summon the gods to their last battle at Ragnarok (*qv*) with his trumpet Gjallarhorn. At the end of the world he will battle his sworn enemy Loki, leader of the powers of Hel (see below). It is predicted that he and Loki will kill each other. Wiser heads say they will take no bets and make none.

HEITSI—*Hottentot*

God of the hunt. He dies and is reborn.

HEL—*German*

Goddess of the furthest section of Niflheim, the place of ice and darkness. The entrance to Hel's area is guarded by a dog of the most foul and uncouth behavior named Garm.

HELEN—*Greek*

Daughter of Zeus and Leda. Helen's suitors were oath-bound to abide by her choice of a husband and to fight those who would oppose this union. But mortals are a tiresome lot and Paris did not respect Helen's choice of Menelaus. The result was the Trojan War. When Troy fell, Helen returned to Menelaus. When he died she was driven from the country and murdered by the queen of Rhodes. Much of Helen's suffering was caused by Paris, who claimed that he loved her. Mortals are like that.

HELIOS—*Greek*

Son of the Titans Hyperion and Theia. Brother of Selene and Aurora. Father of Aeetes, Circe and Phaethon. Helios is omniscient and reports the activities of Earth to the other gods.

HEPHAESTUS—*aka* Hephaistos—*Greek*

Son of Hera. God of volcanoes. An artist of great repute in the field of metal-working, he is known as a respected patron of the arts and crafts. His most celebrated workshop is the Mount Etna Smithy in Sicily where, aided by the cyclopes Zeus assigned there, he creates armor for gods and heroes, the thunderbolts of Zeus and mechanical contraptions of all sorts. Rumor has it that he was lamed when Zeus hurled him from Olympus during a quarrel. Others state that he tripped and fell. Hephaestus rarely speaks about the matter.

HEQET—*Egypt*

The goddess who attends births.

HERA—*Greek*

Daughter of Cronus and Rhea. Sister-wife of Zeus. Mother of Areas, Hephaestus, Hebe and Eileithyia. Queen of heaven. It is said by many that she is a jealous and vindictive spouse. Actually, it's no wonder. The way Zeus behaves is a scandal. Hera is a loving protectress of all women who remain uninvolved in her husband's philandering.

HERAKLES—*aka* Hercules the Hero, Hercules the Great, Hercules the Magnificent, etc., ad infinitum, ad nauseam—*Greek*

Son of Zeus and the mortal Alcmene. As a youth, he went about the countryside killing giants and other innocent creatures and claiming that they were monsters. In his numerous press releases he stated that he was the perfect mortal and was merely righting wrongs.

However, his deeds caused so much commotion and sorrow for all concerned that Hera, in desperation, drove Herakles mad to put a stop to it. However, mistaking his wife and children for Zeus knows what sort of creatures, he slew them too. When Herakles finally recovered his sanity, the Oracle at Delphi advised him to do something useful for a change. Instead, Herakles persuaded the foolish King Eurystheus of Mycenae to assign him 12 labors.

Thus it was that Herakles strangled a sick lion, beheaded a garden snake and severely polluted the Alpheus and Peneus Rivers during a stable-cleaning operation. He also murdered Queen Hippolyta of the Amazons in order to steal her belt. There were a host of other misdeeds.

Hera could take no more. She struck him mad again to put a stop to it. Herakles then murdered the brother of Iole, his intended bride. Hera realized that madness could not stop Herakles, so she restored his sanity. He immediately married some woman named Deianira and took poor Iole as a concubine.

Nessus the centaur finally took matters into his own hands after being accused of the attempted rape of Herakles's wife and then being shot with a poisoned arrow by Herakles. Nessus persuaded Deianira to dip a tunic in his blood and give it to Herakles. It was done and the poison in Nessus's blood entered Herakles's body and caused him to suffer the agonies of Nessus. Herakles jumped into a fire and made an ash of himself.

Zeus, who could be as foolish as most mortal fathers in matters concerning his children, brought Herakles to Olympus. Hera was dead set on throwing him out, but Herakles apologized profusely for all the trouble. Hera said he might as well stay where she could keep an eye on him, so she married him off to Hebe. He has behaved ever since.

HERMES—*Greek*

Son of Zeus and Maia. Father of Autolycus, the great thief. God of travel. God of trade. God of hunting. God of exploring. God of embassies. Messenger of the gods. Protector of travellers, merchants and thieves. Apollo, who fancies himself a bit of an aristocrat, has always looked down on Hermes as "far too earthy to be a decent god, if you know what I mean." This actually stems from Hermes's theft of Apollo's cattle. It wasn't the theft so much, but Hermes hid the herd so well Apollo couldn't find it and Apollo just couldn't forgive that.

HERMOD—*German*

Son of Odin and Frigg. Brother of Balder. Hermod leapt the gate of Hel's domain itself astride his steed to rescue his brother from the land of the dead. He was thwarted by Loki, the Destroyer.

HEROVIT—*aka* Jarovit—*Slav*

God of the army.

HESPERIDES—*Greek*

Daughters of Hesperus. With the assistance of their watch-dragon, they guarded the golden apples Gaea gave Hera as a wedding gift. Herakles the Pest stole the apples and gave them to King Eurystheus the Idiot. It was one of the more pointless things Herakles did.

HINE-NUI-TE-PO—*dba* Hine—*Polynesia*

Daughter-wife of Tane. Goddess of night. Queen of the nether world.

HIPPOLYTE—*Greek*

Daughter of Ares. Queen of the Amazons. Ares loved her so much that he allowed her to wear his golden belt. Herakles slew her and stole the belt from her dead body.

HIRANYAKASIPU—*India*

Father of Prahlada. The demon-king who proclaimed himself king of the universe. It disturbs him greatly that his son is so devoted to the god Vishnu.

HIRANYAKSHA—*India*

A demon that held Earth prisoner beneath the waters of a flood.

HOENIR—*German*

He gave newly created mortals the senses they now enjoy.

HOLDA—*aka* Hulda—*German*

Goddess of beauty and love.

HORAE—*Greek*

They are Eunomia, Dike and Eirene. These goddesses are the gatekeepers of heaven. They are also music lovers and choreographers whose Dance of the Four Seasons is renowned throughout Olympus.

HORUS—*Egypt*

Son of Osiris and Isis. God of the sky and sun.

HOTEI—*Japan*

God of good luck.

HOW-CHU—*China*

God of the air.

HSI-WANG-MU—*China*

The goddess who is the Royal Mother of the Western Paradise. She possesses the herb of immortality and governs the forces of plague and calamity. Her residence is within a mountain of jade.

HU—*Egypt*
The force of creative will.

HUACAS—*Peru and Bolivia*
A natural object with an obvious supernatural manifestation. If this makes no sense to you, you are not paying attention.

HUANG-TI—*China*
The god who invented the compass.

HUITZILOPOCHTLI—*Aztec*
Son of Coatlicue. Brother of Coyolxauhqui and numerous other siblings. God of war. He slew his sister Coyolxauhqui and 400 of his brothers when they would have slain his mother for birthing him. They were concerned, you see, because Huitzilopochtli was born fully armored. In any case, Huitzilopochtli led the mortal Azteca tribe from Astlan to the Lake Texcoco swamps where they founded the great multi-hued city Tenochtitlan. He also renamed the tribe the Mexica.

HUITZNAHUA—*Aztec*
The remaining brothers of the war god Huitzilopochtli who were defeated but not deposed during the power struggle between the war god and his unfortunate sister.

HUNAHPU—*Maya*
Twin brother of Ixbalanque. God of the sun and creator of magic.

HUNAHPU-GUTCH—*Maya*
One of the 13 gods who created human beings. Nothing much good ever comes out of a committee.

HUNAHPU UTIU—*Maya*

Another of the 13 gods who created human beings.

HURACAN—*aka* Hurucan, Hurakan and Hurukan—*Maya*

God of the great storms of summer. God of terror. It was Huracan who flooded the earth while a great fire raged in the sky.

HUVE—*aka* Huveane—*Bushmen of Africa*

The supreme god.

HYADES—*Greek*

Daughters of Atlas and Aethra. When Dionysus was a young god, they were his nurses.

HYDRA—*Greek*

Nine-headed reptilian offspring of Typhon and Echidna. Resided in the marshes of Lerna and was slain by Herakles. Herakles then dipped his arrows in Hydra's blood and thus all wounds caused by those arrows became incurable. Nice fellow, Herakles.

HYDROMEL—*German*

The liquid which gives all who drink it the power of prophecy. The giant Suttung once kept it stored in an underground chamber where his daughter Gunnlod guarded it. It is no longer there, however, and no one is quite sure who does have charge of it at the moment.

HYMENAEUS—*Greek*

Son of Dionysus and Aphrodite. The god of marriage.

HYPERION—*Greek*

Son of Uranus and Gaea, which makes him a Titan. Brother-husband of Theia. Father of Helios, Selene and Eos. Hyperion was so handsome that he was often confused with Apollo by those who did not know either party very well.

IX

IDA, IDA - TEN AND ISSITOQ

IAPTEUS—_Greek_
A Titan. Son of Uranus and Gaea. Husband of Clymene. Father of Atlas, Prometheus, Epimetheus and Menoetius. He currently resides in Tartarus, where he was sentenced by Zeus after participating in the Rebellion of the Titans.

ICARIUS—_Greek_
A mortal who lived in Athens. He welcomed Dionysus into his home without knowing his true identity. Dionysus was so impressed with his host's kind and generous hospitality that he taught him how to make wine. Icarius shared it with his neigh-

bors. They got half-drunk, thought they had been poisoned, and killed Icarius. Dionysius was so furious that he struck every mortal in the entire area stark, raving mad.

ICARUS—*Greek*

Son of Daedalus, a human inventor and architect. Killed while test-flying one of two sets of wings manufactured by his father. Daedalus, who was wearing the other set, claimed the pair were actually escaping King Minos of Crete after their business relationship soured. Daedalus further claimed it was Icarus's failure to exercise due caution that caused the crash. However, Daedalus was wanted on a previous murder charge and later killed King Minos, so there is reason to doubt the claim of accidental death.

ICAUNUS—*Gaul*

The spirit of the Yonne.

IDA—*German*

The countryside around Asgard, famed home of the gods.

IDA-TEN—*Japan*

A handsome young god who protects monasteries. His swift speed of movement is unmatched.

IDOLS.

Statues that intolerant mortals assume are actually thought to be gods. The intolerant mortals call their own idols statues.

IDUN—*German*

Wife of Bragi, god of poetry and eloquence. She is the guardian of the golden apples the gods eat to keep their youth. At one time, Loki and the giant Thjazi kidnapped Idun and took her to Jotunheim,

where the giants dwell. The gods became quite angry
and a fearful Loki brought Idun back to Asgard.
Thjazi flew in hot pursuit, but was shot down in
flames.

IEGAD—*Pelew Islands*
The god who brought light to Earth so that
mortals would have to get up in the morning instead
of sleeping the clock around.

IFA—*Yoruba, Africa*
God of the west. God of secrets. God of divination.

ILLUYANKA—*Hittite*
The great serpent who was slain by the combined
efforts of a storm god and a mortal.

ILMARINEN—*Finland*
The smith god who forged the sun.

ILMATAR—*Finland*
God of the earth.

INANNA—*dba* Ishtar—*Mesopotamia*
The queen of heaven.

INCANTATION—*A prayer.*
I pray, you make incantations, he calls upon
demons to produce heathen deviltry.

INDRA—*aka* Mahendra, Sakra, Satakratu, Pakasasana
and Puramdara—*India*
King of the gods. God of storms. Slayer of
demons. Destroyer of fortresses and compeller of
clouds.

INI-HERIT—*dba* Onuris—*Egypt*
Goddess of mediators, diplomats, statesmen and
conciliators. When the goddess Tefnut became angry
and bore the sun god away, it was Ini-herit who

sought after her, calmed her and returned the sun to the sky.

INTI—*Inca*

Supreme god. God of the sun. Founder of the Inca Empire.

INUAT—*Eskimo*

The spirits who live within all living creatures and who maintain the lamps of life.

IRIS—*Greek*

Daughter of Thaumas and Electra. Sister of the harpies. Goddess of the rainbow. Messenger of the gods. Advisor and guide to mortals.

IRSIRRA—*Hurrite*

Goddess of fate.

ISHTAR—*Babylon and Assyria*

Daughter of Anu the supreme god. Sister-wife of Tammuz. Goddess of love and fertility. Winged goddess of war. Goddess of spring. Goddess of Earth. Queen of heaven. Descended to the underworld to free Tammuz from death and was imprisoned by Queen Ereshkigal. Ishtar refused to be imprisoned. Therefore, she freed herself, rescued Tammuz and went home.

ISIS—*Egypt*

Daughter of Geb and Nut. Sister-wife of Osiris. Sister of Seth and Nephthys. Mother of Horus. Patroness of loving wives and mothers. When Osiris was treacherously slain and dismembered by Seth, Isis searched for the parts of his body and restored him to life. Isis knew everything but the secret name of Re. She has now learned that name and so knows everything.

ISLAND OF FLAME—*Egypt*

The Island of Flame was the first body to appear. Upon it, in turn, appeared eight divinities. They are: Nun and Naunet, god and goddess of the ocean; Heh and Hehet, god and goddess of the immeasurable who created the sun; Kek and Keket, god and goddess of darkness which enables the sun to shine; Amun and Amunet—*aka* Niu and Niut—god and goddess of mystery who are made of air and, as Niu and Niut, invisible.

ISSITOQ—*dba* The Giant Eye—*Eskimo*

The god who seeks out those who break the rules.

ITCHITA—*Yakut*

Goddess of Earth. The goddess who prevents illness. She resides in a high white beech tree.

ITZAMNA—*Maya*

God of water.

IXBALANQUE—*Maya*

Twin brother of Hunahpu. God of the moon. God of magic.

IXMUCANE—*Maya*

One of the 13 gods who created human beings.

IXPIYACOC—*Maya*

Another of the 13 gods who created human beings.

IYATIKU—*Navajo and Pueblo*

Mother of humans. Mother of maize (corn). She brought mortals forth from the womb of the earth where they were created. She gave them her heart, which was maize, and told them it would be their food.

IZANAGI and IZANAMI—*Japan*

Brother-husband and sister-wife. Parents of Amaterasu, Susanowa and Tsukiyomi-no-Mikoto. They are of the eighth generation of the first gods who were born of chaos. They created the Island of Onogoro and dwelt there happily until Izanami died. Her brother-husband sought to bring her back from the Land of Death but she had already partaken of food from that land and was bound to stay.

X

JINN AND JUCK

JAGANNATH—*India*

Lord of the world. Contrary to popular belief, Jagannath is not Juggernaut and he does not dash about crushing whatever is in his path. Once a year, faithful worshippers of Jagannath take his statue and the statues of his brother and sister and mount them on carts which are pulled about. The cart is extremely large and there have been occasional fatalities when careless individuals have slipped and fallen beneath its wheels.

JANUS—*Roman*

God of all beginnings. God of all places of passage. Guardian of gates and doors.

JAR-SUB—*Turkey*

God of the universe.

JASON—*Greek*

A mortal. Son of Aeson, king of Iocolos. Tutored and protected by Chiron the centaur. A protégé of Hera. The gods aided him when he voyaged forth in the *Argo* to seek the Golden Fleece. Jason would have been set for life, but he was unfaithful to his wife Medea. And this after Medea caused her father great sorrow and anger by aiding Jason in obtaining the Golden Fleece. Jason claimed he dumped Medea because he was appalled by her cruel sorcery. The truth is, they had been husband and wife for ten years and Jason became infatuated with Creusa, daughter of Creon. In any case, a raging Medea slew Creon, Creusa and the two sons she bore Jason. Jason himself was killed when a section of the stern of the beached *Argo* fell on him.

JINN—*dba* Djinn, Genii and Genie—*Arabia*

They live on the mountain Kaf and are ruled by King Suleyman. They are made of fire and live, die and give birth much as humans do. However, they are extremely long-lived. They have a good bit of supernatural power, a fine sense of humor and are good at heavy construction work. They assisted in the construction of the pyramids. They can appear in human form when they feel like it and, like mortals, they can be good or bad.

JOLI-TOREM—*Vogul*

Sister of Num, the creator. Goddess of foremen. Joli-torem directed and supervised Num's work so that it would be true and good.

JUCK—*Shilluck, Africa*
Creator of the world.

JUMALA—*Finland*
Supreme god. God of the sky. God who decides how long mortals will live.

JUNO—*aka* Juno Regina, Juno Lucina, Juno Sospita and Juno Lanuvina—*Roman*
Sister-wife of Jupiter. Queen of heaven. Goddess of the moon. Guardian of national finances. Patroness of women. Protectress of childbirth.

JUPITER—*dba* Jove, Jupiter Pluvius and Jupiter Tonans; *aka* Optimus Maximus—*Roman*
Brother-husband of Juno. God of the sky. God of all weather. Guardian of all property. Guardian of oaths and treaties:

JURASMAT—*Latvia*
Goddess of the sea.

XI

KISHIMO - JIN, WHO CHANGED HER MIND

KA—*Egypt*
The soul. A soul is an indwelling divine principle given to all mortals. No one has yet been able to decide if they are truly worthy of it.

KAANG—*aka* Khu, Kho and Thora—*Bushmen, Africa*
The supreme god.

KAIMAI and TRENTREN—*Araucana Indian*
Two serpents who made the seas rise in a great flood to prove how magnificent were their magic

powers. Serpents, you see, can be just as vain and heedless as both gods and mortals.

KALI—*India*

Wife of Shiva. Goddess of destruction. She spurned her husband because he took to drugs and left the protection of the universe to her. She was quite capable of doing the job. She came to Earth to protect humans from demons and slew the general of the demons.

KALKI—*India*

A future god who has not yet appeared. He will be a giant of a man who will put an end to wickedness. Then, all will return to Brahma until it is time to begin again.

KAMA—*India*

God of desire.

KAMMAPA—*Sesuto, Africa*

A monster who fed upon mortals until only one very old woman was left. The old woman bore a child and named it after the god Lituolene. The Kammapa was torn to pieces by Lituolene.

KAREI—*Andaman Islands*

God of storms. God of thunder.

KARTTIKEYA—*aka* Skanda and Scanda—*India*

Son of Shiva and six nymphs. The six-faced god of war who leads the heavenly hosts into battle. He rides a peacock.

KATHAR—*dba* Kathar the Clever—*Ugarit*

God of architects. God of artisans. God of weapon-makers. Kathar built the palace of Baal.

KAUKIS—*Prussia*
Gnomes.

KAZOBA—*Baziba, Africa*
Son of Wamara. Father of Hangi. God of the sun. God of the moon.

KEK—*Egypt*
God of darkness.

KEKET—*Egypt*
Goddess of darkness. See ISLAND OF FLAME.

KELPIE—*Scots*
An ill-tempered water sprite who has only one eye. He lurks in lakes, rivers and the sea. He rushes forth with a terrible roar, snatches his victims and drags them beneath the surface.

KENOS—*Tierra del Fuego*
He was sent to Earth by the supreme god and told to bring order to the world. Kenos created human beings and returned to the sky to await further orders. He is still waiting.

KERI and KAME—*Bacairi Indians*
Twin brothers who created the human race.

KERRIDWEN—*Celtic*
Goddess of inspiration. Goddess of knowledge.

KHADAU—*Amur*
Husband of Mamaldi. With his wife, he was co-creator of the world. But he became upset when Mamaldi created Asia, and killed her. Khadau then continued with the creation of magicians. To annoy him, the dead Mamaldi gave them all souls.

KHENTIMENTIU—*Egypt*
The god who rules the destiny of the dead.

KHNUM—*Egypt*
The god of potters. He is the god of potters because he models bodies of clay and breathes life into them.

KHONS—*dba* Khons Hor—*Egypt*
Son of Amun and Mut. God of the moon. When he appeared at Ombos wearing a falcon's head, several statues were commissioned to commemorate the event.

KHONUUM—*Pygmies, Africa*
Supreme god. God of the rainbow. God of hunters. His bow is made of two serpents and is visible to mortals as a rainbow.

KHOROMOZITEL—*aka* domovoi, domovik, and uboze—*Slav*
Domestic spirits. No, not the alcoholic kind!

KHOSADAM—*Yenisei (Siberia)*
Wife of high god Ec. After she was driven out of heaven for being unfaithful to Ec, she became an Eater of Souls.

KHOVAKI—*aka* Savaki—*Tungus*
Creator of the world.

KHUSOR—*Semite*
God of navigation. God of incantations.

KHWARENAH—*Persia*
It is of fire which dwells in the water. It is destiny and fortune and it is possessed by all mortals, though they know it not. It is forever multiple and changing.

KIANTO—*Lacandon Maya*
God of foreigners and diseases.

KICHIJO-TEN—*Japan*
Goddess of good fortune. Goddess of beauty.

KIGATILIK—*Eskimo*
A fanged demon with no love of priests.

KIHE-WAHINE—*Hawaii*
Goddess of demons. Goddess of lizards.

KINGU—*Babylon*
Husband-son of Tiamat. Leader of the forces of the beginning and shaping of the world when the forces battled the gods.

KISHIMO-JIN—*aka* Hariti and Karitei-mu—*Japan*
Mother goddess of demons. She was once a horror who devoured children and destroyed towns. Finally, she was forced to suffer the anguish she had caused. Once she realized what she had been doing she ceased her evil ways and became the protectress of children.

KOBOLD—*German*
There are two basic types of kobolds. One is a good-natured household sprite who is fond of pranks—some say overly fond—but who will normally help with housework as long as he is properly fed. The other sort of kobold inhabits caves and mines and can become a bit nasty at times.

KOMBU—*Bantu, Africa*
God of creation.

KON—*Peru*
God of the desert.

KORRED—*Celtic*
Dwarves.

KORRIGANES—*Celtic*
Fairies.

KOTTAVEI— *India*
Goddess of war.

KRISHNA—*India*
Avatar of Vishnu. Charioteer of Arjuna. He has quite a way with the ladies.

KUBABA—*Kish*
Mother of Puzur-Sin, first king of the Fourth Dynasty of Kish. The goddess herself, a former barmaid, reigned as queen of the Third Dynasty for 100 years.

KUBERA—*India*
God of wealth.

KUDIA—*Siberia*
God of the sky.

KUEI-HUI—*China*
This is the bottomless pit in the Eastern Sea into which all the waters of this world and of the Han flow. Mortals call the Han the Milky Way. The Five Islands of the Immortals once floated in the Kuei-hui but an incredibly stupid giant sank two of them. The other three islands got loose, floated off somewhere and have not been seen since.

KUL—*Vogul and Ostiak*
Nasty water spirits who dislike sharing their fish with mortals. Not only are they selfish types, they also inflict sickness on mortals at a whim.

KUL-UASA—*Finland*
God of water.

KULLA—*Babylon*
The god who restores temples.

KUMARBIS—*Hurrite*
Father of the gods.

KUMARI—*India*
Virgin goddess.

KUN-LUN—*China*
The Lord of the Sky's capital on Earth.

KURKE—*aka* Curche—*Prussia*
God of corn. No, not maize. There is a difference.

KUSAG—*Babylon*
Patron-god of priests. He is the god who is the high priest of the gods.

XII

LILITH, LOKI AND LUGEILAN

LADA—*Slav*
Goddess of beauty.

LAHAR—*Sumer*
God of cattle.

LAIMA—*Latvia*
Goddess of childbirth.

LAIMA—*Lithuania*
Fairies of fate.

LAKSHMI—*India*
Wife of Vishnu. Goddess of beauty. Goddess of wealth. She is a very fickle woman who claims that no god can sustain her for long.

LARES—*Roman*

Minor gods of protection. Lares permarini guard sailors and those who travel by sea. Lares compitales guard crossroads. Lares militares guard soldiers. Lares semitales guard footpaths and byways. These are only a few of the better-known lares. There are several dozen more.

LATMIKAIK—*Pelew Islands*

Wife of Tpereakl. Goddess of the sea. Co-creator and co-ruler of the world.

LAUKAMAT—*Latvia*

Goddess of the fields.

LAUKOSARGAS—*Prussian*

God of the fields. God of grain.

LAUME—*Prussia*

Goddesses of protection. They reside on Mount Laumygarbis in the province of Natangia, Prussia.

LEMURIA—*Roman*

The period from May 9 to May 13 when hungry spirits prowl around dwelling-places at night.

LEPRECHAUN—*Celtic*

A small fairy who prefers to go about looking like an elderly mortal male. Leprechauns are well known for their fine leather work; the shoes they craft are among the finest known. It is rumored among humans that a leprechaun will divulge the location of his life savings if captured by the commanding glare of a mortal gaze. However, when bullied and threatened by thieves, leprechauns have meted out stern punishment.

LETHE—*Greek*

The River of Oblivion which flows through the underworld. Those who drink of the water become amnesiacs.

LETO—*Greek*

Daughter of Coeus and Phoebe. Mother of Apollo and Artemis. A Titan. Her difficulties during childbirth are legendary. Apollo and Artemis were not the problem. Hera was. She was so jealous of Zeus's affair with Leto that she prevented the goddess of childbirth, Eileithyia, from going to Leto for nine days. After nine days of labor, Leto was exhausted. To save her, the other goddesses bribed Eileithyia to disobey Hera.

LEVIATHAN—*Phoenicia*

A serpent-monster who inhabits the deeps. It must be noted that the Phoenicians were excellent mariners and they knew whereof they spoke.

LIA FAIL—*Celtic*

The Stone of Destiny. It was brought to Ireland by the Tuatha De Danann and was placed at the Hill of Tara. Upon this stone are crowned the kings of Ireland. The voice of the stone will groan its mighty approval when a worthy king rides across it. It will remain silent if the ruler is unworthy.

LIBITINA—*Roman*

Goddess of funerals.

LILITH—*Hebrew*

First wife of Adam. Rejected because she was not quite human. Now known as the queen of demons.

LISA—*Fon, Africa*

Son of Nana Buluku. Twin brother of Mahu. Father of Dan. God of the sun. God of the sky. God of power.

LLORONA—*Spain*

A female spirit who lures people to their death by drowning in bogs and ponds. Normally she does this by waiting until the dead of night and weeping and crying like a frightened child.

LLUD—*aka* Nudd or Nuada—*Celtic*

Son of Dana and Beli. The god whom London was named in honor of. The city's original name was Caer Ludd and the temple of Llud was atop Ludgate Hill.

LLYR—*aka* Ler or Llediaith—*Celtic*

Father of Bron (or Bram) and Manannan (or Manawydan). God of the sea.

LODUR—*German*

The god who gave mortals the warmth of life.

LOKI—*German*

Son of Farbauti and Laufia. Father of Hel, the Fenris wolf (see FENRIR) and the Midgard Serpent. God of strife, evil, discord and other nasty things. He is a handsome fellow with a small, agile build. He also has no sense of honor and is amoral. His behavior was so abominable that he was chained with ten chains and will stay that way until the Twilight of the Gods, when he will break loose and destroy everything.

LOPEMAT—*Latvia*

The goddess who created cattle.

LORELEI—*German*

A beautiful singer who inhabits the Rock of the Lorelei on the right bank of the Rhine River near St. Goar. She has not been seen since mortals bored a hole through her rock. The mortals claimed the rock was a hazard to navigation and blamed the Lorelei every time they ran into it.

LUCINA—*Roman*

Goddess of childbirth.

LUGEILAN—*aka* Luk—*Caroline Islands*

Son of Aluelop. God of knowledge. He taught mortals the arts of tattooing and hairdressing.

LUGH—*dba* Lug, Lamh-fhada and Samhoklanach—
Celtic

God of sorcery. God of poetry. God of history. God of carpenters. His magic lance is not guided by a hand; it strikes the enemies of the god Lugh of its own will. No mortals can bear to look upon Lugh because he is so radiant.

LUNA—*Roman*

Daughter of Hyperion. Goddess of the moon.

LUPERCUS—*Roman*

God of flocks and fertility. Protects sheep from wolves. His feast is the Lupercalia.

LUXOVIOUS—*Gaul*

Consort of Bricta. God of the waters of Luxeuil.

LYCAEUS—*Greek*

The mountain where Zeus was born.

XIII

MAGIC, MANASA AND MOSCHEL

MAAT—*Egypt*
Daughter of Re. Goddess of truth and justice. Weigher of souls. She is the order which rules the worlds through balance.

MAB—*Celtic*
Fairy queen of Connaught. Goddess of dreams.

MAGIC
A form of science which is not acceptable to scientists because they are unable to explain it.

MAGNI—*German*

Son of Thor. Brother of Modi. A future god who has not yet come.

MAH—*Persia*

An assistant to Vohu Manah of the Amesha Spentas. Mah has been given the task of presiding over time and tide.

MAHASAKTI—*dba* Mahesvari, Mahakali, Mahalkakshmi and Mahasarasvati—*India*

The Divine Mother. Supreme creator of the universe. Goddess of war, wisdom and passion. Her work is perfect and her force can shake worlds. She is the most gentle and delicate of goddesses.

MAHU—*Fon, Africa*

Daughter of Nana Buluku. Twin sister of Lisa. Mother of Dan. Supreme goddess of the earth. Goddess of the moon. Goddess of fertility.

MAHUIKA—*Polynesia*

The goddess who rules the edges of the underworld.

MAIA—*Greek*

Daughter of Atlas and Pleione. Mother of Herakles by Zeus.

MAKUNAIMA—*Carib Indian*

Brother of Manape. Creator of the heavens, animals and humans. Makunaima and his brother pulled down the Tree of Life, thus flooding the earth with water. It was not a total disaster. The floodwaters spread plants all over the globe.

MAMALDI—*Amur*

Wife of Khadau. Co-creator of the earth. She was killed by her jealous husband for creating Asia.

However, she continued to annoy him by creating souls for the magicians he built.

MAMI—*Babylon*
Mother goddess who created mortals.

MANALA—*dba* Tuonela—*Finland*
The underworld. It is inhabited by giants of various races as well as those mortals who are dead and awaiting rebirth. The giants know quite a bit about medicine and can often provide remedies for illnesses.

MANANNAN MAC LLYR—*Celtic*
Son of Lyr. God of the capes of the sea. God of storms and waves. God of merchants. God of fishermen. His ship follows his command without sails; his cloak makes him invisible; his helmet is of flames and his sword cannot be turned from its mark.

MANASA—*India*
Queen of serpents. Manasa grants fertility to sterile mortal females. The serpents (Nagas or Naginis) will confer spiritual truths upon deserving humans.

MANCO-CAPAC—*Inca*
God of fire.

MANES—*Roman*
Spirits of the dead.

MANIBOZHO—*Algonquin Indian*
God who created the earth and mortals. This was not his original intent. Manibozho flooded the universe to put out a fire started by his enemies. He created the earth and humans from the mud that was left behind after the flood. He also taught his creation how to survive.

MANITOU—*dba* The Great Spirit—*American Indian*
The spirit that rules all things. The master of life.

MANTCHU-MUCHANGU—*Shongo, Africa*
God of dressmakers. He taught humans how to make clothes and cover their bodies.

MARA—*Norse*
A goblin which seizes male mortals in their beds and takes away all speech and motion.

MARAWA—*Melanesia*
He made human beings mortal because he was unfamiliar with their basic construction.

MARDUK—*Babylon*
The supreme god. God of the sun. Leader of the gods.

MARISHI-TEN—*Japan*
Goddess of warriors. Goddess of first light. She is invisible and rules the light that appears in the sky before the sun. She guards warriors against the weapons of their enemies.

MARS—*Roman*
Consort of Rhea Sylvia. Father of Romulus and Remus. God of war. God of the beginning and ending of battles. God of agriculture. God who protects the field against plant diseases. He is the father of the Roman people, which explains a great deal about the Roman people.

MARSYAS—*Asia Minor*
Son of Hyagnis. A Sileni (woodland satyr) who was flayed to death by Apollo for playing one of Athena's cast-off flutes. Gods do not always know how to share gracefully.

MATH—*Celtic*
Brother of the goddess Dana.

MATRONAE—*Celtic*
The three mother-goddesses who oversee fertility. They are lovers of peace, tranquility and children.

MAUI—*Polynesia*
Son of the sun. God of fire. God of islands. Maui gave mortals the gift of fire and made the days longer for them. At one time, he fished an island from the deep sea, where islands are hard to come by.

MEIDEN—*Lithuania*
God of animals. God of forests.

MELKART—*aka* Melqart—*Phoenicia*
God of travelers. God of sailors. God of colonies. God of the city of Tyre. Melkart is, like the Phoenix, regenerated by fire.

MELPOMENE—*Greek*
Daughter of Zeus and Mnemosyne. Muse of Tragedy.

MELUSINA—*France*
Daughter of the fairy Persine and Helmas, King of Albania. Wife of Raymond, Count of Toulouse. A beautiful female who is subject to becoming a mermaid at times. She does not like to be seen while undergoing metamorphosis, and when Raymond accidentally saw her, she became upset and vanished. He, being mortal, has since died. Melusina, who is not, is still seen at Lusignan Castle. Humans believe that she appears clad in mourning to warn royalty of impending calamity.

MERCURIUS—*dba* Mercury—*Roman*
God of commerce. Messenger of the gods.

MERLIN—*aka* Myrddin—*Celtic*

Merlin refuses to reveal his parentage. However, it is widely rumored that he is the son of a god and a mortal princess. He is Lord of Fairyland. He is the mightiest of prophets and maintains a sincere humility and deep love for all living creatures. He is in the wood Broceliande.

MERMAIDS—*Chaldean*

Sea-dwellers with the bodies of mortal women and the tails of fishes.

MEZAMAT—*Latvia*

Goddess of forests.

MEZAVIRS—*aka* Mezadevs—*Latvia*

God of forests.

MICHABON—*Ottawa Indian*

The god who created mortals from animals.

MICLANTECUTLI—*Aztec*

God of the dead.

MIDEWIWIN—*Algonquin Indian*

The Great Medicine Dance which guards the tribe in matters of safety, health and wealth.

MIDGARD—*German*

The fortress that humans call Earth. It was created by Aesir (gods) to protect mortals from the Jotnar (giants). The Aesir live in the center of Midgard in an area called Asgard.

MILK—*Gilyaks, Siberia*

Devils.

MIMIR—*Norse*

Son of Aegir, the god of the calm sea, and Ran, the goddess of the stormy sea. God of wisdom. He dwells in Mimir's Well, which is located in the open sea.

MIN—*Egypt*
God of procreation. God of fertility.

MINABOZHO—*Algonquin Indian*
The god who fell into the sea and caused it to overflow.

MINERVA—*Roman*
Daughter of Jupiter and Juno. Virgin goddess of warriors. Goddess of poetry. Goddess of medicine. Also goddess of painting, teaching, dyeing, spinning, weaving, sewing and wisdom. Inventor of musical instruments and numbers.

MINGA BENGALE—*Shongon, Africa*
God of hunters. God who taught humans how to make nets.

MINOS—*Crete*
Son of Zeus and Europa. King of Crete. He ruled a marvelous kingdom but he was a bit of a spoiled brat. Thus, he came to a bad end.

MINOTAUR—*Crete*
Son of a bull of Poseidon and Pasiphae, wife of King Minos of Crete. He is half bull and half man, or so the gossip goes.

MIRABICHI—*Ottawa Indian*
God of the water.

MIRACLE
A supernatural event produced by the god or goddess currently in power. When produced by any other god or goddess it is called witchcraft.

MIRMIR—*German*

An uncle of Odin's. He is the guardian of the fountain of wisdom and intelligence.

MISOR—*Semite*

The god who created salt.

MITHRA—*Persia*

God of soldiers. God of war. God of justice, order and discipline. God of heavenly light, including the sun. God of contracts. God of restraint.

MITRA—*India*

God of light and truth. God of joy, love and life. Co-guardian (with Varuna) of the laws by which the universe is maintained and nature is made fruitful.

MIXCOATL—*Aztec*

Star god. God of the hunt. Serpent of the clouds.

MNEME—*Greek*

One of the original three Muses (their number was later increased to nine). Sister to the Muse of Song, Aoide, and the Muse of Meditation, Melete. Mneme is the Muse of Memory.

MNEMOSYNE—*Greek*

Daughter of Uranus. Mother of the nine Muses of Zeus. Goddess of memory.

MNEUIS—*aka* Mnevis—*Egypt*

A sacred bull.

MODI—*German*

Son of Thor. Brother of Magni. A future god whose time has not yet come.

MO-HI-HAI—*China*

God of water.

MOIRA—*aka* Moirai and/or Moerae—*Greek*
The fates.

MOKOS—*dba* Mokusa—*Slav*
Goddess of sheep. Goddess of those who spin wool.

MOLOCH—*Ammonite*
God of fire.

MONOS—*Greek*
God of sarcasm. God of pain.

MONTH—*Egypt*
The god of Thebes who fell into disfavor with mortals due to royal politicking during the Eleventh Dynasty. The disgusted Month has not been heard from since.

MORGANES—*Celtic*
Female water spirits.

MORPHEUS—*Greek*
Son of Hypnos (*dba* Somnus) the god of sleep. Morpheus is the god of dreams.

MORRIGU—*aka* Morrigan, Badb, Macha and Nemain—*Celtic*
Goddess of war. Queen of ghosts.

MOSCHEL—*Latvian*
God of cows.

MOT—*Ugarit*
God of the netherworld.

MUGASHA—*Baziba, Africa*
Son of Wamara. God of water.

MU-KING—*China*
God of fire.

MUSPELSHEIM—*German*

Dwelling of the sun. A southern land of fire. The sparks from the fire of the southland became stars after the gods set the vault of the heavens over the world.

MUSSO KORONI—*Bambara, Africa*

Daughter of the Voice of the Void. Wife of Pembu. Goddess of disorder.

MUT—*Egypt*

Wife of Ammon, or Amon, or Amen, or any other spelling he feels like. Mother of Khonso (Khons). Mother goddess. Queen of heaven.

MYTHOLOGY

1. A defunct religion. 2. A religion held in disbelief by the person discussing it.

MYLITTA—*Babylon*

Goddess of fertility. Goddess of childbirth.

XIV

A FEW WORDS ABOUT NYMPHS

NAGA—*India*

A non-violent race of serpents who are benevolent toward humans. The Naga king can be depended upon to assist in matters concerning peace, justice, fertility, health, spiritual enlightenment and wealth.

NAHUAL—*Aztec*

Nahuals are protectors of mortals. Each mortal has a nahual which is created of the same stuff as the mortal.

NAHUI OCELOTL—*Aztec*

The first sun, called the tiger sun, which lasted 676 years. At the end of that time, the inhabitants of the planet Earth were eaten by tigers and the sun vanished. Nahui Ehecatl, the second sun and the wind sun, then appeared. It lasted 364 years. At the end of that time, horrible winds scoured humans from the face of the earth. Those few who survived became monkeys. Then came Nahui Quiahuitl, the third sun and rain sun, which lasted 312 years. Fire fell from the sky, destroying all, and humans were changed into birds. Next followed Nahui Atl, the water sun and the fourth sun. It continued for 676 years and then a flood destroyed the world. Humans became fish and only one mortal man and woman survived. The fifth sun is Nahui Ollin. It is the earthquake sun. It is our sun.

NAIADS—*Greek*

Female fresh water spirits. They live in fountains, springs, wells, rivers and lakes. The waters wherein they dwell have curative powers and can create a temporary prophetic condition.

NAJADE—*Slav*

Water nymphs.

NAMMU—*Sumer*

Mother of the Gods. Creator of heaven and earth. She brought organization to the world of mortals.

NANA BULUKU—*Fon, Africa*

Father of the twins Mahu and Lisa. Supreme god.

NANAHUATZIN—*Aztec*

Father of the sun. God of courage and bravery. Nanahuatzin was a small leper-god who was told it was his job to light the sun. He had no offerings to give for this task, so he threw himself into the flames. Thus was the sun born.

NANNA—*German*

Daughter of Nip. Wife of Balder. Goddess of purity. Goddess of vegetation. When Balder died, Nanna fell dead at his side. They are buried in the same grave.

NARAYANA—*India*

The soul of the universe.

NARCISSUS—*Greek*

Son of Cephissus, the river god. A handsome and exceedingly vain fellow who felt no love for anyone other than himself. Some say it was for love of him that poor Echo pined away. In any case, Nemesis was annoyed because Narcissus loved nothing save himself and so caused much pain to others. She caused him to fall in love with his own reflection. So great was his vanity, that he was unable to stop gazing lovingly at himself. He starved to death, which served him right.

NAREAU—*Gilbert Islands*

Lord Spider. Creator of the universe.

NAV—*Slav*

Spirits of mortals who died tragically and too soon.

NDEGEI—*Fiji*

Serpent god. He hatched the bird's egg from which mortals emerged. He creates earthquakes.

NDYAMBI-KARUNGA—*aka* Kalunga and/or Nzami—
   Bantus and Hereros, Africa

Husband of Mutifi. God of the sky. God of the sea. God of earth. God of rain. God of law. God of the dead. God of growing crops.

NECROMANCY

Annoying the dead by calling them back to life to answer silly questions.

NECTAR—*Greek*

Drink of the immortal Olympian gods. This drink gives immortality. It is said to resemble red wine, but it has a most delicious scent.

NEFERTUM—*Egypt*

Son of Ptah and Sakhmet. God of the sun. This young god often went about with a lotus flower on his head. This gave rise to the quaint mortal notion that the sun was actually a lotus flower.

NEHALENNIA—*German*

Goddess of navigation. Goddess of commerce.

NEITEROGOB—*Masai, Africa*

Goddess of Earth.

NEITH—*Egypt*

Mother of the gods.

NEKKER—*aka* Nikker—*German*

A water sprite who appears to sailors to warn them that they are in danger of death by drowning.

NEMAIN—*Celtic*
Goddess of panic.

NEMAUSUS—*Gaul*
Spirit of the Spring of Nimes. He was later promoted to god of the city of Nimes.

NEMESIS—*Greek*
Virgin goddess of law, retribution and punishment.

NEPTUNE—*Roman*
Son of Saturn and Rhea. Brother of Jupiter and Pluto. God of the sea.

NEREIDS—*Greek*
The 50 daughters of Nereus and Doris. They are Mediterranean Sea nymphs who spend their time on the sea bottom and surface only to aid sailors fighting perilous storms. Nereids are also able to prophesy.

NEREUS—*Greek*
Son of Pontus and Gaea. Husband of Doris. Father of the Nereids. God of the Mediterranean Sea. He is able to foretell the future and is prone to shape-changing.

NERGAL—*Babylonia and Assyria*
Supreme ruler of the land of the dead. God of the midsummer sun. God of war. God of pestilence. God of the chase.

NERTHUS—*German*
Goddess of fecundity. Goddess of peace. Goddess of wealth. For some reason, she goes about among mortals. She claims she likes them.

NESR—*aka* Nasr—*Arabian*
Vulture god.

NEURI—*Slav*
A race of sorcerers who change into wolves for several days once each year.

NGA—*Yurak (Siberia)*
The god who organized the world after it was created. God of death.

NGAI—*Masai*
Supreme god. God of the sky and of rain and clouds.

NGAKOLA—*Sudan*
Brother of Tere. God of life. He bestowed life on human beings by breathing it into them.

NEGOOGUNOGUMBAR—*Pygmy*
An ogre who swallows children.

NIDHOGGR—*German*
An evil-tempered serpent-dragon who eats the roots of Yggdrasil, the World Tree.

NIFLHEIM—*German*
A northern land of ice, mist and darkness.

NIKE—*Greek*
Daughter of Pallas and Styx. Sister of Zelos, Kratos and Bia. Goddess of victory.

NIMSIMUG—*Babylon*
The god who completes construction.

NINDURRA—*Sumer*
Daughter of Enki and Ninmu. Mother of the goddess Utto by Enki.

NINHURSAG—*aka* Nintue, Ninmah and Aruru—
Sumer
High goddess. Goddess of mountains.

NINIB—*Babylon and Assyria*
God of the spring sun. God of the morning sun.

NINILDU—*Babylon*
Another god who completes construction.

NINMU—*Sumer*
Daughter of Enki and Ninhursag. Mother of the
goddess Nindurra by Enki.

NIO—*Japan*
Spirits who protect children, prevent thefts and
chase away evil from monasteries. They are ugly and
threatening in appearance, but you will rarely find
nicer spirits.

NIOBE—*Greek*
Daughter of Tantalus. Wife of Amphion, co-
governor of Thebes. Mother of either 12 or 14 children, depending on whom you ask. Currently, one
cannot ask Niobe. Her vain presumptions of superi-
ority so angered Zeus that he turned her to stone.
Her children are dead.

NIU—*dba* Amun—*Egypt*
God of mystery.

NIUT—*dba* Amunet—*Egypt*
Goddess of mystery.

NIX—*aka* Nixie—*German*
Freshwater spirits with human bodies and the
tails of fish. They can assume other shapes when they
feel like it and they can also become invisible.

NJORD—*German*

Husband of Skadi. Father of Freyr and Freyja. God of the sea. God of sailors. God of fishermen. God of fertility. His ship, Skidbladnir, is quite large. However, it can be folded up and carried about in a pocket.

NOMMO—*Sudan*

The twins, one daughter and one son, of Yurugu, god of sailors. The Nommo sailed down the rainbow in an ark carrying all living creatures.

NONADEY—*Lithuania*

Leader of the gods.

NORNS—*German*

The best-known of the Norns are the three young women, Urd, Verdandi and Skuld, who sit by the Well of Urd under the World Tree Yggdrasil in Asgard where they determine the fate of gods and mortals. Urd knows the past, Verdandi the present and Skuld the future. There are many other minor Norns, both good and evil, who possess the arts of prediction and magic.

NU-KUA—*aka* Nu wa Niang Niang—*China*

The goddess who created the human race. Her basic material was yellow mud. When evil set fire and flame loose upon the world, Nu Wa set the world aright and melted stones of five colors to repair a rent in the sky.

NUBA—*Sudan*

God of the sky.

NUDIMMUD—*Babylon*
The god who created the first ocean.

NUJALIK—*Eskimo*
Goddess of the land-hunt.

NUM—*dba* Num-torem—*Samoyed*
God of the sky. Supreme first-god. The god who created land from the water with the help of a diving bird. He is made of fire and humans are unable to look at him. His home is in the Seventh Heaven and he stores the Water of Life there.

NUN—*Egypt*
God of the ocean. It is also the nothing which contains everything and from which all life came.

NUNET—*Egypt*
Goddess of the ocean.

NUSMATLIWAIX—*Bella-Coola Indian*
The cave in which all the rivers and riverdwellers of the world were imprisoned. The entrance was barred by a huge rock. It was Raven who broke the barrier and freed them all.

NUSKU—*Assyria*
Son of Sin. God of fire. God of light. God of civilization. Messenger of the gods.

NUT—*Egypt*
Daughter of Shu and Tefnut. Sister-wife of Geb. Mother of Osiris, Isis, Seth and Nephthys. Goddess of the sky.

NYALITCH—*aka* Nyalic—*Dinka, Africa*
Supreme god. Lord of spirits. God of the sky. God of rain.

NYAME—*aka* Nana or Nyankopon—*Ashanti, Africa*

Husband of Asase Ya. God of rain. God of the wind. God of the sun. God of the moon, night and sleep.

NYIA—*Slav*

The god of the dead.

NYIKANG—*Shilluck, Africa*

God of ancestors. God of agriculture. God of rain. He is the intermediary between humans and gods. He can change animals into humans. He instituted the practice of marriage and then vanished in a whirlwind.

NYIKO—*Cameroon*

Son of Nyokon and Mfan. God of divination. He was driven from heaven by his father.

NYOKON—*Cameroon*

Husband of Mfan. Father of Nyiko. Supreme god.

NYMPHS—*Greek and Roman*

They are lesser goddesses of great beauty who are loved and respected by gods and sensible mortals. Among the classes of nymphs are: Dryads and Hamadryads who live among trees in forests; Oreads who dwell in mountains and grottoes; Limoniads, who prefer meadows and flowers; Limniads which are found in the vicinity of lakes, marshes and swamps and who can be dangerous to travelers; Napaea who can be sought out in valleys where herds graze; Oceanids who live in streams and fountains; Nereids who are the daughters of Nereus; Potameids who abide always in rivers which are not overly polluted; Pleiades who are the seven daughters of

Atlas and Pleione; Atlantids who are the offspring of Atlas; Naiads who can live in any liquid element (but only there) and the Hyads, who have been changed to stars.

NYX—*Greek*

Daughter of Chaos. Goddess of night. Goddess of darkness.

NZAMBI—*aka* Nzame, Nzakomba, Djakomba and Mbomba—*Bantu*

Supreme god. God of creation. Nzami created the first man and named him Fam. Fam grew vain and destroyed the earth. Nzambi buried him in a hole and created Sekume. Sekume was a far better creation and even managed to make his own wife, Mbongwe, from a tree.

NZEANZO—*Sudan.*

God of rain. God of fertility. God of medicine. God of metal-working. God of corn.

XV

OANNES TO OYA

OANNES—*aka* Annedotus, Anementos, Odakon and/
or Euedokus—*Babylon*

The god of the sea. During the day he lives with
humans and instructs them in the arts and sciences.
At night he retires to the Erythraean Sea, which is
currently called the Persian Gulf. Berossus, priest of
Bel, says Oannes has the head and body of a fish and
the feet of a man. Other sources who are equally as
reliable as Berossus say Oannes has a human head. It
is quite likely that Oannes appears in whatever fash-
ion he fancies at the moment.

OBATALA—*Africa, Carbibbean, South and Central America*

The most powerful of all gods. He alone knows the hiding place of the Great Almighty.

OBERON—*aka* Alberon and Alberich—*Europe*

Husband of Titania. King of the elves. When he blows his horn, all wicked persons must dance.

OBI—*aka* obe and obeah—*Africa and West Indies*

A form of witchcraft which is often used for antisocial behavior. However, in the hands of the proper person, it can also be a powerful source of good.

OBTALA—*Yoruba, Africa*

Son of Olorun and Olokun. Father of Aganju and Yemaja who gave birth to Orungan who impregnated his mother. She gave birth to Dada, Schango, Ogun, Ochossi and Schankpannan. Obtala is the God of the North.

OCEANIDS—*Greek*

Daughters of Oceanus and Tethys. At latest count, there are 4,000 of these ocean nymphs.

OCEANUS—*Greek*

Son of Gaea and Uranus. The oldest of the Titans. He is of the ocean and has willingly given his name to it.

OCCULT

Unconventional religion. Once a religion becomes conventional, it is no longer considered to be occult. This is known as scientific truth-seeking.

OCHUN—*aka* Caridad, the Lady of Charity—*Africa, South and Central America and the Caribbean*

Queen of the Sweet Water.

ODIN—*dba* Woden, Wodan, Wode and Wuotan—
German

Son of Bor and Bestla. Brother of Vili and Ve.
Husband of Iord, Frigg and Ring. Ruler of the world.
Oldest of the gods. God of sailors. God of storms.
God of science and inventions. God of battles. God of
poetry, writing and magic. Leader of the Wild Hunt,
which crosses the world like a firestorm in the night.
He is missing an eye and has been known to go
among mortals disguised as the poorest of the poor
seeking aid. His two raven messengers are Huginn
and Muninn. His two wolves are Geri and Freki. His
eight-footed steed is Sleipner.

ODUDU—*Yoruba, Africa*

Son of Olokun and Olorun. Brother of Obtala.
God of the South.

OENGUS—*Celtic*

Son of Dagda. God of love. No one can resist
music from Oengus.

OENONE—*Greek*

Wife of Poris. A nymph of Mount Ida. A prophetess who warned Paris against taking the journey
which resulted in the abduction of Helen and led to
the Trojan War.

OGMIOS—*aka* Ogma and Ogma Sun-Face—*Celtic*

God of eloquence. It is he who invented the runic
language of the Druids.

OGRIGWABIBIKWA—*Pygmy, Africa*

A dwarf who changes into a reptile.

OGUN—*Africa, South and Central America and the*
Caribbean

God of warriors.

OGYRUAN—*Celtic*
Father of Gwenhwyar. God of bards.

OHONAMOCHI—*Japan*
God of the earth.

OKUNI-NUSHINO-MIKOTO—*Japan*
God of medicine. God of fishing. God of the raising of silkworms and the art of silk-making.

OKUNINUSHI—*Japan*
Son off Susanowo. The god who built the non-celestial world.

OLOFAD—*Caroline Islands*
Son of Lugeilan and a mortal female. Messenger of Lugeiilan. God of fire. God of singing and dancing.

OLOKUN—*Yoruba, Africa*
Wife of Olorun. Mother of Obtala and Odudua. Goddess of the primordal water.

OLORUN—*Yoruba, Africa*
Husband of Olokun. Father of Obtala and Odudua. Supreme god.

OMECIUTAL—*Aztec*
Wife of Ometecuhtli. Mother of Tezcatlipoca the Red, Tezcatlipoca the Black, Tezcatlipoca the White and Texcatlipoca the Blue.

OMEN
An extraordinary occurrence which presages a coming event.

OMETECUTLI—*Aztec*
God of fire.

OMOPHAGIC RITES
Cannibalism. It still isn't nice.

OPHIOLATRY
Serpent worship. Serpents are associated with fertility, resurrection and immortality. The rumor that ophiolatrists are demon-worshippers is calumny.

OPS—*Roman*
God of harvests.

ORACLES
Responses given by a god to a worshipper. They are commonly called answers to prayers.

ORCUS—*Greek*
God of oaths. Punisher of perjurers. He is often confused with Pluto. This is odd, as the two don't look a bit alike.

OREADS—*Greek*
Nymphs of mountains and grottoes.

ORKO—*Basque*
God of thunderstorms.

ORMUZD—*aka* Ormazd, Ahura Mazda and Auramazda—*Persia*
God of the sun. Guardian of humankind. Head of the Heavenly Host.

OROMILA—*Benin, Africa*
The spirit of divination.

OSCHUN—*Yoruba, Africa*
Wife of Schango. Goddess of rivers. Goddess of food.

OSIRIS—*Egypt*
Son of Geb and Nut. Brother-husband of Isis. Brother of Seth and Nephthys. Father of Horus. God of the flood. King of the gods. God of the lower world. God of agriculture, law and learning.

OT—*Mongolia*
Goddess of marriage. Queen of fire.

OURANOS—*Phoenicia*
God of fire.

OYA—*Yoruba, Africa*
Wife of Schango. Goddess of violent storms. Goddess of the River Niger. Goddess of fertility.

XVI

PAN, PEREPLUT AND PINGA

PACCARI TAMPU—*Peru*
The House of the Dawn. It is a cave south of Cuzco on the Vilcamija River where Manco Capac and his brothers first appeared on earth.

PACHA-MAMA—*Peru*
Goddess of the earth.

PACHACAMAC—*Yuncas* (No not the Incas. They came later.)
Supreme god. Creator. God of the earth.

PALES—*Roman*

Guardian of flocks and sheep. Pales is worshipped sometimes as a goddess and sometimes as a god. Pales does not particularly care which.

PALLADIUM—*Greek*

The statue of Pallas which fell to earth from heaven.

PAN—*Greek*

Son of Hermes. God of flocks. God of fertility. God of nature. Leader of the satyrs in their revels. Has been known to cause an unreasoning terror, known as panic, in a flock of sheep. Did the same to the Persian Army at the Battle of Marathon and thus became a favorite among Greek mortals. Pan is half man and half goat with goat horns. He loves mountains, caves and lonely places where he can practice his pipes without disturbance. Prefers to sleep until noon and becomes furious if disturbed.

P'AN KU—*China*

Born in the egg of chaos. He is a giant who became the world. His voice is thunder, his breath is the wind and his tears are rivers.

PANDORA—*Greek*

First mortal woman. Manufactured to order by Hephaestus for Zeus, who was temporarily angry at all mortal males then inhabiting the earth. The other gods and goddesses were genuinely delighted with Pandora and bestowed many useful gifts upon her. Zeus, with a great show of paternal benevolence, gave Pandora a gift-wrapped parcel and told her to wait until reaching earth before opening it. The box was full of trouble.

PAPA—*Polynesia*

Wife of Rangi. Goddess of earth. Goddess of fertility.

PARIACA—*Peru*

The god who flooded the earth with water because mortals were unkind to him.

PARTHENOPE—*Greek*

A siren who fell in love with Odysseus and who cast herself into the sea for love of him. She washed up on the shores of a small Italian village, which took her name. Later, for reasons now unknown, it changed its name to Naples. Its luck has been spotty since then.

PARVATI—*aka* Uma, Ma Kali, Durga, Bhairavi, Ambika, Sati and Gauri

Daughter of the Himalayas. Wife of Siva. Destroyer of demons. Dancer of the Cosmic Dance.

PAX AUGUSTA—*Roman*

Goddess of peace.

PEGASUS—*Greek*

Created from sea foam by Poseidon. A winged horse who made his first appearance near the source of the ocean. Captured at the Pirene Spring (now a fountain in the city of Corinth, Greece), by Bellerophon, who rode him to war. Pegasus creates springs by striking the earth with his hooves. He amuses himself by chasing thunderbolts hurled by Zeus and returning them.

PELIAS—*Greek*

Son of Poseidon and Tyro. He drove his younger stepbrother from the throne of Iolcus and was killed by Medea.

PEMBO—*Bambara, Africa*

Son of the Voice of the Void. Husband of Musso Koroni. God of wisdom. God of water. God of agriculture.

PENATES—*Roman*

The generic name for household divinities. Each household has its own penates. There are also public penates who guard communities.

PENTHESILEA—*Greek*

Daughter of Ares and the Queen of the Amazons. She fought on the side of the Trojans during the Trojan War. She was slain in battle by Achilles, who grieved deeply for her.

PEREPLUT—*Slav*

Goddess of drink. Goddess of changing fortunes.

PERI—*Persia*

Spirits of great beauty who guide mortals on their way to the Land of the Blessed. They also battle evil daevas (*qv*).

PERKUNIS—*Slav*

God of thunderstorms.

PERSEPHONE—*Greek*

Daughter of Zeus and Demeter. Wife of Hades. Hades abducted Persephone from a meadow and took her to the lower world, where he made her his wife. Demeter could not be consoled and wandered the earth weeping and seeking her daughter. Nothing would grow while Demeter wept. When Demeter located Persephone, there was some negotiation and Hades agreed to have Persephone spend spring and summer with her mother and return to him in the fall and winter.

PERSEUS—*Greek*

Son of Zeus and Danae. He cut off the head of the gorgon Medusa, who was minding her own business at the time, and gave the head to Athena. This disgusting homicide won him acclaim and honor.

PERUN—*aka* Perkunas Peroun—*Slav*

God of thunder and lightning. God of water. God of the oak.

PHAETON—*Greek*

Son of Helios. A spoiled child who stole his father's chariot. He drove it so wildly through the heavens that he set the earth aflame and all life was endangered. Zeus felled him with a thunderbolt in order to preserve everyone from incineration.

PHLEGETHON—*Greek*

One of the five principal rivers of the kingdom of Hades. It is a tributary of the Styx, as are Acheron, Cocytus and Lethe, but they are merely water. Phlegethon flows with fire which burns and does not consume.

PHOENIX—*Asia*

A bird which has a lifespan that ranges from 500 to 1,000 years. It is voluntarily consumed by fire and then arises young and restored from its own ashes.

PINGA—*Eskimo*

Healer of the sick. Goddess who guards the souls of the living. Guardian of game. It is she who instructs the moon god Alignak as to when to return the souls of the dead to Earth for rebirth.

PIRITHOUS—*Greek*

Son of Zeus and the mortal Dia. A ne'er-do-well who, after several misadventures, descended to the lower world to steal Persephone, the wife of Hades, for his bride. Pirithous felt it would be perfectly all right to do so, as he was half-god and therefore deserving. However, he was apprehended by the local authorities and chained in the infernal regions. He is still there today.

PLEIADES—*Greek*

Daughters of Atlas and Pleione. They are seven sisters and are called Electra, Taygete, Maia, Alcyone, Celaeno, Merope and Asterope.

PLUTO—*Greek and Roman*

Son of Kronos and Rhea. Ruler of the lower world. Judge of dead mortals.

PLUTUS—*Greek*

Son of Iasion and Demeter. God of wealth. Zeus blinded him so mortals would not be judged too harshly as to their worthiness to hold wealth. This accounts for the fortunes amassed by undeserving scoundrels.

POLUDNITSAPRZYPOLUDNICA—*Slav*

A very small spirit of the Summer Wind.

POLYPHEMUS—*Greek*

Son of Poseidon. One of the Cyclopes. He was a one-eyed, cannibalistic giant. After he met Odysseus he became a blind, cannibalistic giant.

POMONA—*Roman*

Goddess of fruit trees. Goddess of fruit.

POPUL VUH—*Quiche Maya, Guatemala*

A history book which details the story of Xbalanque and story of the Creation.

POSEIDON—*Greek*

Son of Kronos and Rhea. Husband of Halia and Amphitrite. Father of Rhodus, Polyphemus, Pegasus, Orion and several other children. God of earthquakes. God of the sea and shore. God of islands. The trident he received from the Cyclopes can make the earth shake. Poseidon's greatest wish is to be named the patron of a city. This has never happened.

PRAHLADA—*India*

Son of the demon-king Hiranyakasipu. Father of Bali. Devoted to the god Vishnu, and for this reason his father tried to slay him. He failed. Instead, Vishnu slew Hiranyakasipu and Prahlada became demon-king.

PRAJAPATI—*India*

Supreme god. Principle of Cosmic Life. Creator of the universe and all its creatures. The act of creation so exhausted him that there was danger he could not sustain what he created. Upon learning this, all the creatures of the universe fled Prajapati, leaving him without joy and food. To save himself and thus save creation, he captured and ate 11 animals.

PRITHIVI—*India*

God of Earth.

PROMETHEUS—*Greek*

Son of Iapetus and Clymeme. Light-bearer. Rebel against unjust authority. He supported Zeus in the

Titan War, but then angered him by stealing fire from Mount Olympus and giving it to mortals. Zeus punished him fearfully for it, but relented in time.

PROTEUS—*Greek*

The Old Man of the Sea. Prophet and shape-changer. He is of great age and wisdom. He pastures the seal-herds of Amphitrite.

PTAH—*aka* Phtha—*Egypt*

Son of Nun. Father of the gods. Creator of Earth. God of law and justice. God of metal-workers and sculptors. He is so short of stature that he is often mistaken for a child. This amuses him.

PURUSHA—*India*

Born of a golden egg. The Purusha has a thousand faces, a thousand eyes and a thousand feet. He is the entire universe—future and past. He is the universe and he inhabits it and sometimes it hurts.

PUSAIT—*Lithuania*

A wood spirit who is often attended by kaukis (gnomes).

PUSHAN—*India*

God of growth. Restorer of what is lost.

PYTHON—*Greek*

The child Gaea conceived after the Flood. Python was/is an enormous serpent which formerly guarded the Oracle of Delphi at Mount Parnassus. Python was slain by Apollo, who then took possession of the oracle. Gaea then promised Python a second chance.

XVII

QAHOLOM AND QUIRINUS

QAHOLOM—*dba* Cajolom—*Maya*
God of the sky. One of the seven gods who assisted in the creation of the world and the formation of human beings.

QAT—*Melanesia*
God of darkness. God of the tides. God of rain. God of the seasons. Created trees, pigs and human beings.

QAT—*Buryan*
Lesser divinities who dwell on the highest mountain peaks.

QUETZALCOATL—*aka* Ehecatl, Yolcuatl, Tohil and Huemac—*Mexico*

God of air, clouds and wind. God of medicine and the healing arts. God of fertility and wealth. God of thieves. God of gambling. God of fishermen. Messenger of the gods. Patron of farmers, planters, gardeners and others who work with the soil. Patron of stone engravers and cutters and of builders. Patron of gold and silversmiths and of all who work with metal. Inventor of books and writing. Inventor of the calendar. He came to visit mortals from Tlapallan, the Bright Land. Humans remarked upon his fair skin and hair and remembered him as the Fair God. He departed to Tlapallan on a boat of serpents, promising to return at an unspecified future date.

QUINAMETZIM—*Tlaxcala, Mexico*

The giants who inhabited the earth in the distant past, as mortals count it, and who warred against mortals.

QUIRINUS—*Roman*

God of war. God of soldiers. Quirinùs, Jupiter and Mars formed the Great Triad of Gods.

XVIII

THE PECULIAR PUNISHMENT
OF RAHU

RAASHIEL—*Semite*
God of earth.

RADOGAST—*Slav*
God of the sun.

RAGNAROK—*German*
The day of doom when the world will perish and be annihilated. It will then be reconstructed as imperishable.

RAHU—*India*

Brother of Ketu. A star demon. Rahu stole the nectar of immortality. He was captured and beheaded before he could swallow it. Thus the body of Rahu perished and his head became immortal.

RAJ—*Slav*

God of the earth.

RAMA-CHANDRA—*India*

Half-brother of Bharata. Husband of Sita. God of moral virtue.

RAMPANOHITAOLANA, RAMPANAOHOZATRA, RAMPANAHODITRA, RAMPANAORA and RAMPANELOMBELONA—*Madagascar*

The five members of the Zanahary gods who shared the work of creating mortals.

RANGI—*Polynesia*

Husband of Papa. God of the sky. God of life.

RANGIDIMADO—*Madagascar*

A creature constructed by one of the Zanahary sky-gods. He became vain and offensive in the eyes of the Zanahary and was dumped on earth and condemned to stay. His friend Razanjanahary was unable to obtain pardon for him, so he helped him with the initial work of creating mortals to keep him company. Several other Zanahary also became interested in this project.

RAPHAEL—*Semite*

God of air.

RASOALAO—*Madagascar*

Sister of Ravola. Goddess of wild animals. Goddess of the hunt. She is a member of the Vazimba gods.

RATATOSK—*German*

The squirrel who forever darts up and down the World Tree Yggdrasil, managing to keep both the eagle at its top and the dragon-serpent at its base in a constant uproar.

RAUNI—*Finland*

God of fertility.

RAVANA—*India*

A demon of the Rakshasa class. Rakshasas are attendants of Kubera, god of riches. Like others of this class, he can assume any shape at will. His normal form is that of a giant with ten heads, 20 arms and a nasty disposition. He is immune to the powers of gods and demons, but he was sorely wounded and thought to be dead after being attacked by an army of monkeys and bears. Ravana brought this upon himself by abducting Sita, the wife of Rama.

RAVOLA—*Madagascar*

Sister of Rasoalao and also a Vazimba god. Goddess of tame animals. Goddess of cattle-raising.

RAZANA—*Madagascar*

Ancestors who have become gods.

RAZANAJANAHARY—*Madagascar*

Son of Andriamanitra and a Zanahary sky-god. Assisted in the initial work of creating mortals.

RE—*dba* Ra—*Egypt*

God of the sun. King of gods and mortals.

REDIYAS—*Semite*

God of water.

RENENUTET—*aka* Thermuthis—*Egypt*

Goddess of abundant harvests.

RESHEF—*Egypt and Canaan*
God of war.

RHADAMANTUS—*Greek*
Son of Zeus and Europa. God of justice. He laid the foundation of the Cretan Code of Law. He was later named a judge in the Islands of the Blessed.

RHEA—*Crete*
Daughter of Uranus and Gaea. Sister-wife of Cronus. Mother of Zeus, Hades, Poseidon, Hera, Hestia and Demeter. Goddess of earth. Her favorite hobby is taming the most ferocious of wild beasts who then follow her with love and devotion. Rhea maintains that it is merely a matter of love and respect.

RHIANNON—*Gaul*
Mare goddess. Great Queen.

RIG VEDA—*India*
An ancient book that instructs how the gods punish by permitting.

RISHI—*India*
Sages who spring from the mind of Brahma and become demigods.

ROBUR—*Gaul*
God of oak trees.

ROC—*Persia*
A ferocious bird of enormous size. It is able to carry away an elephant in its talons. One feather from its body is as large as the longest frond on a full-grown palm tree.

ROD—*aka* Rozanitsa and Rodienitsa—*Slav*
Demons of fortune, destiny and judgment.

RONGO—*Polynesia*
God of fertility. God of agriculture.

RUDRA—*dba* Siva and Nilakantha—*India*
Husband of Parvati. God of violence. Healer of all wounds. Those who oppose him, he destroys.

RUGEVIT—*Slav*
The seven-faced god of war.

RUSALKI—*Slav*
The spirits of women who die before marriage and then become water sprites.

RUSSALKA—*Russia*
Protectresses of national heroes. They are beautiful, long-haired females who are winged. They possess eternal youth, beautiful voices and unusual power.

RYANGOMBE—*Baziba, Africa*
Son of Wamara. God of cattle.

XIX

SATYRS AND SERAPHIM

SAGBATA—*Fon, Africa*
A member of the Vodu gods family. God of earth.

SAKHMET—*Egypt*
Mother-goddess of Memphis.

SALMONEUS—*Greek*
Son of Aeolus, the wind god. Salmoneus was king of Elis, which should have contented him. It didn't. He felt destined for better things. When the populace demanded rain, Salmoneus stated that he could provide it. He tied bronze kettles to his chariot to imitate the sound of thunder and dragged them

about throwing torches in lieu of lightning bolts and shouting loudly that he was Zeus and it had better rain or else. Aeolus was terribly embarrassed. When Zeus finally stopped laughing, he fried Salmoneus with a thunderbolt and nearly drowned Elis in a downpour.

SAMAIN—*Celtic*
New Year's Eve and New Year's Day.

SAMPO—*Finland*
An instrument which grinds out prosperity.

SAMPSA PELLERVOINEN—*Finland*
God of planting and sowing.

SARASVATI—*aka* Satarupa, Savitri, Gayatri and Brahman—*India*
Goddess of science. Goddess of wisdom. Goddess of music. Inventor of the alphabet. She was born of Brahma's self. It was for her love that he created the world.

SATYRS—*Greek*
Young male fertility spirits. They have the legs and tails of goats, the heads and torsos of humans and pointed ears with small horns. They are fond of wine and are somewhat lustful. However, they are also refined and personable young divinities who love to dance with the nymphs.

SATURN—*Roman*
Husband of Ops. Companion of the Fire Goddess Lua. Father of Picus. God of seed time and harvest. He reigned during the Golden Age and shared his throne with Ops.

SATURNALIA—*Roman*

The feast celebrating Saturn's rule. It is generally held December 17-23. During Saturn's rule, freedom and equality reigned and violence and oppression were not found. During Saturnalia, public business ceases, masters and slaves exchange places and gift-giving, feasting and other things frowned upon by oppressive religions take place.

SAVITRI

The creator of immortality.

SCAMANDER—*aka* Xanthus—*Asia, vicinity of Turkey*

A small stream with two sources, one hot and one cold. It has a curiosity value.

SCARAB—*aka* Scarabaeus sacer—*Egypt*

The sacred beetle of immortality.

SCORPIUS—*Greek*

The scorpion which slew Orion the hunter by stinging him in the foot. It is a normal reaction by scorpions when they are trod upon by those who do not look where they are going. Nevertheless, there were hard feelings. When the gods placed Orion and Scorpius in the sky they were separated as far as possible so that they would never meet again.

SCYLLA—*Greek*

A monster with 12 feet, six necks and six mouths. She resides on a rock on the Italian coast. When she is in residence, navigation in the area is extremely hazardous.

SE—*Fon, Africa*

Supreme god.

SEA SERPENT

The first recorded sighting of one by mortals was made by Norse sailors in Scandinavian waters. The gentle sea serpent has a long and slender neck and a wide body. Despite wild tales told by humans, attacks by sea serpents are extremely rare. These creatures are repelled by mortals, fear them, and seek to flee them.

SEDNA—*Eskimo*

Goddess of the creatures of the sea. Mortals claim that she is fat, hideous, ill-tempered, etc., etc., etc. However, the sins of these very mortals tangle her hair and those who do not hunt with respect for the hunted cause her terrible pain. When Sedna is treated with honor, gentleness and the strength of honesty, she provides food for mortals.

SEDRAT—*Arabia*

The lotus tree which stands on the right-hand side of the throne of Ali. Countless angels rest in the shade of this tree and two rivers run from its roots.

SEGOMO—*Gaul*

God of war. God of victory.

SELKIS—*Egypt*

Goddess of scorpions. Guardian of coffins. She resides in the scorching heat of the sun and her beauty lives forever.

SEMIRAMIS—*Assyria*

Daughter of Derceto of Ascalon, the Syrian fish-goddess. Goddess of love. Goddess of war. When she ruled Assyria, she built Babylon and its famed hanging gardens. She also led mighty war campaigns against Persia, Egypt, Libya and Ethiopia.

SEQUANNA—*Celtic*
A river goddess.

SERAPH
An extremely ancient divinity. It is human in form but has three pairs of wings. Humans often claim that seraphim cover their faces with one pair of wings, their feet with the other and use only the mid-wings for flight. However, seraphim are not particularly adept at flying blind. Actually, when upper and lower wing pairs are not needed for strenuous flight, they are folded down for a streamlining effect.

SERAPIS—*dba* Sarapis—*Egypt*
The god who cures the sick. Although he is an Egyptian god, he is not generally accepted by the Egyptians. Serapis does not like to discuss the subject.

SETH—*Egypt*
Son of Geb and Nut. Brother of Isis, Osiris and Nephthys. God of storms. A nasty sort who killed his brother to attain power.

SHADRAPHA (*pseud.*) Shed the Healer—*Phoenicia*
God of healing.

SHAHAR—*Ugarit (Syria)*
Son of El. Brother of Shalim. The gracious god.

SHAMAN
A mortal who is a healer, educator, war-chief, lawyer and judge. It is amazing what uneducated and superstitious sorts have said about shamans.

SHAMASH—*dba* Samas—*Babylonia and Assyria*
Son of Sin-Nanna. Husband of A. Father of Kettu and Mesharu. God of the sun. God of justice. God of healing.

SHANGO—*Yoruba, Africa*

Son of Obtala. Husband of Oya, Oshun and Oba. God of the east. God of war. God of thunder.

SHAPH—*Ugarit*

Goddess of the sun. She helped Anat bind and carry Baal to the top of Tsaphon where he will resume his glorious reign.

SHELVA—*Toltec, Mexico*

The giant who escaped the Great Deluge by climbing the mountain belonging to the god of water. When the waters subsided, Shelva built the pyramid of Cholula.

SHIVA—*aka* Siva, Rudra, Nataraja and 1,000 other names—*India*

God of time. God of justice. God of water. God of the sun. The Destroyer, Shatterer of Worlds. The Creator, Regenerator of Worlds. He is red-haired and resides on Mount Kailas, northernmost peak of the Himalayas.

SHOTEN—*dba* Daisho-kangiten—*Japan*

God of gamblers. God of prostitutes. God of merchants and speculators. God of procurers. God of actors and geishas. If prudence and proper form are not used when worshipping Shoten, unremedial ruin shall flow upon the head of the offender.

SHU—*Egypt*

Son of Atum. Brother-husband of Tefnut. Father of Geb and Nut. God of air.

SIBYL

Sibyls have fallen upon hard times lately. However, in the ancient world they were widely respected as prophetesses and their abilities were renowned. It is the ancient Sibylline prophecy that the world will be destroyed by fire.

SIF—*German*
Wife of Thor.

SIGOO—*Arawak Indian*
God of mercy. It was he who took the animals and birds to the high mountains so that they could survive the Great Flood.

SILA—*Eskimo*
God of energy. God of air. God of movement. God of curing. Ill mortals can be brought back to health when Sila shares his substance.

SILENUS—*Greek*
Companion of Dionysus. His rough and quite uncouth exterior hides great wisdom. He is the keeper of secrets and an extraordinary prophet. He is also obese, bald, bearded, pug-nosed, aged and generally drunk. For all of this pose, he is much beloved by those who know him. He also has the ears, legs and tail of a horse, although he is not a centaur. The centaurs normally give him a ride home when he is in no condition to walk.

SILVANUS—*Roman*
God of uncultivated land. Those who wish to clear and plow land must first receive Silvanus's permission. Otherwise, no crops will grow.

SILVER AGE—*Roman*
The historical period during which Jupiter reigned.

SIN-NANNA—*aka* Sin—*Babylon*
God of the moon.

SINGBONGA—*Birhors, Central India*

The god who created the earth. He created the winged horse, then he created humans.

SIRENS—*Greek*

Sea nymphs who prefer to live on out-of-the-way islands. They enjoy raising their sweet voices in songs of celebration of the beauty of the world. Mortal sailors who pay more attention to the nymphs than to their sailing and navigation often pile their ships straight onto rocks and reefs. Then they blame the nymphs.

SIRONA—*Gaul*

Goddess of astronomy.

SITA—*aka* Parthivi—*India*

An incarnation of Laksmi, goddess of love, prosperity and learning.

SMAJ—*Serbia*

Protectors of the Serbian nation. These divinities resemble winged male mortals and have been known to shoot fire while flying.

SOBK—*Egypt*

The Crocodile God of Faiyum.

SOLAL—*Caroline Islands*

Brother of Aluelop. God of the underwater world. Keeper of the First Rock from which the world was made. Creator of the earth and sky.

SOMA—*India*

The moon god. Soma has also given his name to a reddish plant with a golden sap. Just a few drops of this juice, carefully pressed from the plant, will bestow great strength and courage.

SOMNUS—*Roman*
Son of Nox. Father of Morpheus. God of sleep.

SOUL
The non-material presence which animates life. Among some religions, it is held that only human beings have an immortal soul and that the souls of all other life perish when the host body dies. This violates Einstein's Theory that matter and energy are interchangeable and never lost.

SPHINX—*Egypt*
Spirit-guardians of entrances. There are several species of Sphinx: The Ram-Headed Lion, the Hawk-Headed Lion and the Human-Headed Lion. Sphinxes of all species are said to love riddles.

SPOR—*Slav*
The spirit of growth.

SRAOSH—*aka* Srosh—*Persia*
A divine messenger and mediator between gods and mortals.

STRIBORG—*Slav*
God of winter.

STYX—*Greek*
Daughter of Oceanos. Mother of Zelos, Bia and Kratos. Goddess of oaths. Styx dwells in a lovely grotto at the entrance to Hades. At her urging, her children aided Zeus in the Titan War. For this assistance, Zeus decreed that an oath was not properly witnessed unless the name of Styx was attached to it.

SUDJAJE—*Slav*
Female divinities who control destiny.

SUKUNA-BIKONA—*Japan*
A dwarf who came by boat to assist Okuninushi in building the world.

SUPAY—*India*
God of air.

SURYA—*India*
God of proper action.

SURYASAVITRI—*India*
God of the sun. God of light. God of truth.

SUSANOWO—*aka* Susa-No-O—*Japan*
Son of Izanagi. God of water. God of storms. God of the sea. For all of this, he has the manners of a slob.

SUSSISTINNAKO—*Sia Indian. North America*
The Great Spider Sussistinnako was the first of all living creatures. It was not until he shook his magic rattle and sang that the other living creatures came forth.

SVAROG—*dba* Svarozits—*Slav*
God of fire. God of the sun.

SVATOG—*Slav*
God of the atmosphere.

SVETOVID—*aka* Svantovit and/or Svantevit—*Slav*
Chief of the gods. God of fate. God of fertility. God of war.

SWASTIKA
The ancient symbol of all sun gods. Mortals who have attempted to divert this symbol to their own

causes have created grave disasters, chaos and a multiple of other evils.

SYLPH

Elemental spirits of the air. They are swift, transparent and have foreknowledge. They also eat, drink, speak, bear children and become ill.

SYLVANUS—*Roman*

God of rural areas. He is half man and half goat.

XX

THE REVENGE OF TAKARO

TAGES—*Etruscan*

A small demon who, for reasons known only to himself, appeared to mortals in a newly plowed field. He lived among them for some time, instructing them in the proper methods of interpreting the signs sent by the gods.

TAGUACIPA—*Inca*

God of deception. He meddled in the creations of the gods, including that of mortals and their planet.

T'AI SHAN—*China*

God of life. God of fate. God of destiny. God of death.

TAKARO—*New Hebrides*

A divinity who forbade anyone to eat coconuts. Another divinity named Mueragbuto ate coconuts for spite. This so vexed Takaro that he forced Mueragbuto to eat coconuts until he died of surfeit of them.

TAKSHAKA—*India*

King of the Naga serpents. He was both crafty and heroic in his deeds while serving as king and is now beloved by Indra.

TALOCAN—*Aztec*

Home of the gods.

TAMMUZ—*aka* Dumu-zi and Adonai—*Babylon*

God of the sun.

TANDU—*India*

One of the principal attendants of Shiva. Tandu is primarily a teacher of mimicry and dancing.

TANE—*Polynesia*

Son of Papa and Rangi. God of forests. God of birds.

TANGAROA—*dba* Ta'aroa, Upao and Vahu—*Samoa and Tahiti*

God of the sea. God of the sky. He created the earth by breaking the Great Egg in half. Then he created the first woman.

TANIT—*Carthage*

Wife of Baal Hammon.

TANO—*Ashanti, Africa*

Son of Asase Ya and Nyame. God of rivers. God of thunder.

TARANIS—*Celtic*

God of thunderstorms.

TAREYA-WAGON—*Mohawk Indian*

The god who liberated the Kaniengehaga, better known as the Mohawks, from confinement beneath the surface of the earth. He then led them to the Valley of the Mohawk on the surface of the planet.

TARTARUS—*Greek*

Son of Aether and Ge. Father of Typhoeus. It is also the deep pit which extends just a bit farther than the universe. In this pit are imprisoned Cronus and the Titans.

TAWHIRI—*Polynesia*

Son of Papa and Rangi. God of winds. God of storms.

TECCUCIZTECATL—*Aztec*

God of the moon. He originally volunteered to light the sun. However, his sacrifices, although costly, failed because he was afraid to sacrifice himself.

TEFNUT—*Egypt*

Daughter of Atum. Sister-wife of Shu. Mother of Geb and Nut. Goddess of rain. Goddess of moisture.

TELAVEL—*Lithuania*

The star-god who forged the sun and placed it carefully in the sky.

TELEPINUS—*Hittite*

God of vegetation. One day he was dozing so soundly that he had to be stung awake by a bee. This happened near the town of Lhizina and the bees there still speak of it today.

TENGRI—*Mongol*

God of the sky.

TEPEU—*Maya*
God of the power in the sky. One of the seven gods who assisted in creation.

TERE—*Sudan*
Brother of Ngakola. The god who gave plants and animals to human beings.

TERPSICHORE—*Greek*
The Muse of Dance.

TESHUB—*Hittite*
Consort of Khepat. God of thunderstorms. Owner of the storm bulls Sheri and Khurri.

TEUTATES—*dba* Alborix, Caturix, Loucetius and Rigisamos—*Gaul*
God of war.

TEXCATLIPOCA—*Aztec*
The supreme god who was created in the formation of the world. God of rulers. God of the north. God of cold. God of darkness.

THALIA—*Greek*
The Muse of Comedy and Pastoral Poetry.

THEMIS—*Greek*
Daughter of Uranus and Gaea. Consort of Zeus. Mother of the Horae and the Moirae. Goddess of law and order. Relentlessly pursues all those who trespass upon the rights of others. She is also a prophetess.

THEOLOGY
A rational discussion about gods. This is a contradiction in terms.

THEORIS—*aka* Thoeris—*Egypt*

Goddess of women in childbirth. Protectress of babies.

THESMOPHORIA—*Greek*

Three-day festival of Demeter the Lawgiver which begins on October 24. Only women are permitted to attend the celebration. Males must stay home and mind the children.

THETIS—*Greek*

Daughter of Nereus and Doris. Wife of Peleus. Mother of the mortal hero Achilles. A sea nymph.

THOR—*aka* Donar—*German*

Son of Odin. Husband of the giantess Iarnsaxa, who bore him Magni and Modi. His second wife is Sif, mother of son Loride and daughter Thrud. God of thunder. God of rain. Sworn to protect mortals against giants. Thor's hammer Mjollnir returns to his hand after it is thrown. It is an extremely short-handled hammer because Sindri, the dwarf who forged it, made a slight miscalculation. Thor currently resides in the Bilskirnic Palace. He is easily irritated and can roar in a terrifying voice, but he is a benevolent type who is a strong friend of peasants and yeomen.

THOTH—*Egypt*

God of time. God of the moon. God of writing, science and medicine. Secretary of the gods. He invented alchemy and magic. He has assisted mortals by writing many works of science, in particular books on astronomy, mathematics and medicine. In fact, this noted writer is the author of 42 books.

TIAMAT—*Sumer*
Goddess of the sea.

T'IEN—*dba* Shang Ti—*China*
Ruler of the gods.

TIKI—*aka* Ti'i—*Marquesas and Society Islands*
Created by Tane. God of virility. Messenger of the gods.

TILO—*Baranga, Africa*
God of the sky. God of rain. God of storms. God of humor. God of cunning. God of mystery. He is the god of twins, who must be called the Sons of the Sky.

TINIA—*Etruscan*
God of fire. God of thunderstorms.

TIRAWA—*Pawnee Indian*
The Great Father.

TITANS—*Greek*
The 12 children of Uranus and Gaea. Male issue: Oceanus, Creus, Coeus, Iapetus, Cronus and Hyperion. Female issue: Rhea, Mnemosyne, Theia, Themis, Tethys and Phoebe. The children of the original 12 are also Titans. However, Zeus and the rest of the Olympian gods prefer to be called Olympians and are the children of Cronus and Rhea. This puts the Titan War, or Titanomachy, into the class of a family squabble.
The Titanomachy began when Uranus banished two other groups of his children, the Cyclopes and the Hecatoncheires, to Tartarus. It is not exactly a pleasant spot. Gaea was incensed and urged the rest of the Titans to oppose this outrage. Cronus attacked Uranus, won, set himself in his father's place and

canceled the order of banishment. Zeus and the rest of the Olympians attacked Cronus, with the aid of the Titans Oceanus and Prometheus. Zeus won and the rest is history.

TLALOC—*dba* Nahualpilli—*Aztec*
God of rain. God of agriculture. God of fire. God of the south.

TLALTECUHTLI—*Aztec*
God of Earth.

TLAUIXCALPANTECUHTLI—*Maya*
God of the dawn.

TLOQUENAHUAQUE—*Aztec*
The unknown god.

TODOTE—*Samoyed (Siberia)*
God of evil. God of death.

TONANTZIN—*Aztec*
The Mother-Goddess.

TONATIUH—*Aztec*
God of the sun. God of warriors. Those who die in his service are rewarded with eternal life.

TOPIELCE—*Slav*
Spirits who dwell in the waters of lakes.

TORE—*Pygmy*
God of thunderstorms.

TOREM—*aka* Torum—*Ugrian*
God of the sky. God of order and balance.

TORTALI—*New Hebrides*
Husband of the mortal Avin. God of the sun. God of the day. His marriage did not work out; mixed marriages between gods and mortals rarely do.

TOYO-UKE-HIME—*Japan*
    Goddess of agriculture.

TPEREAKL—*Pelew Islands*
    Husband of Latmikaik. God of the sky. Co-creator of the world. Co-governor of the world.

TRIGLAV—*Slav*
    God of the sky. God of the earth. God of the lower regions. God of impartial justice. God of judgment. Triglav also has three heads.

TRIPURASURA—*India*
    A demon of three worlds.

TRITON—*Greek*
    Son of Poseidon and Amphitrite. Father of the Tritons. God of the sea. He has green hair and eyes, a human torso and the tail of a dolphin (the mammal, not the fish; Triton knows the difference, even if you don't). His conch horn controls the action of the waves. A soft note sounded by the horn calms the seas and a loud blast sets them crashing about wildly.

TROIAN—*Slav*
    The god of night.

TROLLS—*Norway, Iceland and Scandinavia*
    The Norse claim trolls are gnomes. The Icelanders say their trolls are giants. Scandinavians disagree and state that all the trolls they have ever seen are dwarves. They are all correct, as trolls vary greatly in size. They live underground and are usually quite kind to mortals. However, they have an unfortunate tendency to steal women, children and food. It is difficult to capture them, as they can see the future and become invisible.

TSOEDE—*Sudan*
   God of canoe builders. God of smiths. God of fertility.

TSUI—*Hottentot*
   God of sorcerers. God of rain. God of thunder.

TSUIKIYOMI-NO-MIKOTO—*Japan*
   Son of Izanagi. God of the moon.

TU—*Polynesia*
   Son of Papa and Rangi. God of war.

TUATHA DE DANAAN—*Celtic*
   The followers of the goddess Dana. With the help of Dagda, Gobniu and Lug, they defeated the old gods. When the Tuatha De Danaan were in turn defeated by the new god, they retreated to the hills of Ireland and the fairy folk.

TUIL—*Kamchatka Peninusula, Siberia.*
   God of earthquakes. He rides his sleigh beneath the earth. Tuil can be convinced to go elsewhere with his sleigh by poking holes in the ground with a very sharp stick of the proper length.

TULUNGUSAQ—*Eskimo*
   God of creation. It is said of Tulungusaq that he found life in a dead silver sky and created animals, mortals and light. He then taught the mortals how to hunt and fish and build boats and houses. This done, he returned to the sky and began creating stars. He is still working on this portion of the job, which is why astonomers always find something new to play with.

TUNG-AK—*Mongol*
   God of managers. God of chiefs. Tung-Ak controls minor spirits, as someone must keep their behavior in check.

TUNGAT—*aka* Tug'ny'gat, Tungrat, Tunrat, Tornat and/
or Torngrat—*Eskimo*

Spirits of places and ancient animals. They have great power and hold the secrets of the universe. They are extremely dangerous to human beings. They are also as ugly as they are dangerous.

TUNGRANGAYAK—*dba* Torngarsoak, Tornarsuk or Tornatic—*Eskimo*

The wisest of the Tungat. He sees all but only reveals the cause of illness. He also rules the sea and game.

TUPAN—*Guarani, Brazil*

God of thunder. God of lightning.

TYPHON—*aka* Typhoeus—*Greek*

Son of Tartarus and Gaea. Father of Cerberus, Chimaera and Hydra. Typhon is not particularly attractive. He has 100 snake-shaped heads. They each have eyes that shoot fire and mouths that roar. He also has 50 pairs of hands and a like amount of pairs of feet. His temper matches his appearance. Quite some time ago, Typhon lost his temper and attacked Zeus. Zeus picked up Mount Etna and dumped it on top of him. Typhon is still underneath the mountain and not too happy about it.

TYR—*aka* Ziu, Tiwaz, Tiuz and Tiw—*German*

God of courage. God of honor. God of the unbroken word. God of faithfulness. God of law. God of war. He shares with Odin the duty of choosing the heroes the Valkyries transport to Valhalla. Tyr has one hand. The other was bitten off by the Fenris wolf, Fenrir (*qv*). Fenrir was deceitfully bound by a magic dwarf-forged ribbon. Tyr placed his hand in the wolf's mouth as a pledge that he would be released. When the other gods refused to release him the wolf bit off Tyr's hand.

TZAKOL—*Maya*
   God of the sky.

XXI

ULU TOJON, GOVERNOR OF THE NORTHEASTERN SECTION OF THE UNIVERSE

UGA-JIN—*Japan*
God of the waters. God of the fertility of the earth. He is a serpent god.

UKEMOCHI—*Japan*
Goddess of food. Goddess of sustenance.

UKKO—*Finland*
God of air. God of thunderstorms.

UL—*New Hebrides*

God of the moon. God of the night.

ULGAN—*Siberia*

Supreme god of heaven.

ULL—*German*

God of hunters. Odin was banished as head god for ten years because of his womanizing. During that period, Ull replaced him.

ULLIKUMMIS—*Hurrite*

Son of Kumarbis. He is a terrible monster of diorite who terrified even the gods, as he grew to a height of 27,000 miles. Matters became critical when he stated that he was going to slay mortals. The gods were forced to do battle with Ullikummis and they were a bit surprised at their ability to whittle him down to size.

ULU TOJON—*Yakut (Siberia)*

God of thunder. God of fire. God of magicians. Mortals refer to him as the Great White Creator. He is a stranger who lives in the third heaven. He is the governor of the northeastern section of the universe and rules the Abaasy who live there.

UMA—*aka* Bhavani, Devi, Durga, Kali and Parvati—*India*

Goddess of female creative energy. She is splendid and she is both terrible and kind.

UMAI—*aka* Ymai and Mai—*Turkey*

Goddess of fertility. Goddess of fire. Goddess of the home. Goddess of the hearth. She is golden haired.

UMUNMUTAMKU—*Babylon*

The deity who presents the offerings to the gods after they have been made by humans.

UMUNMUTAMNAG—*Babylon*

Another deity who does the same thing as Umunmutamku.

UNDINE—*Roman*

A female water spirit who is purported to marry mortals in order to acquire a human soul. However, why an Undine would want two souls, her own and that of some mortal, is quite beyond the understanding of the divinities involved.

UNICORN—*India*

Although not a horse, it is of the general size of one and there is a close resemblance. Unicorns have white bodies and blue eyes. The 18- to 36-inch-long horn in the center of a unicorn's forehead is white at the base, black in the center and red at the pointed tip. Those who drink from the hollow horn shed by a unicorn during the natural process of growth, are protected against epilepsy, stomach trouble and poison. Those who cause a unicorn to be slain, grind up its horn and drink it in a potion, have convulsions, stomach cramps and die of poison. Unicorns are fleet-footed and hard to catch. But a contemplative mortal, silently pondering the grandeur of nature in a forest glade, is quite likely to be approached by one of these curious beasts. Those who offer a unicorn no harm will find the creatures quite gentle and friendly. Those who offer a unicorn harm are usually stoned to death by wood nymphs.

UNKULUNKULU—*Kaffir*

Son of Unvelingange. Creator of civilization. He is an impatient type and is indirectly responsible for death because he couldn't wait for the message of creation to be spread among mortals. He chose the messenger. He could have chosen better.

UNVELINGANGE—*Kaffir*

The god who existed before anything else.

UPELLURIS—*Hurrite*

Tred lightly. He is the creature upon whose shoulders the gods placed the world.

URANIA—*Greek*

Daughter of Zeus and Mnemosyne. The Muse of Astronomy.

URANUS—*Greek*

Son of Gaea. With his mother-wife he is the father of the Titans, the Cyclopes, the Olympians and others. First father of the gods.

USHAS—*India*

Goddess of truth. Goddess of light. She wakes the gods from their sleep. She is both young and ancient and she cannot die.

USMA—*Babylon*

Two-faced attendant of Ea, god of the deep sea.

UTNAPISHTIM—*Babylon*

A mortal who was made a god. When the gods sent the Deluge, Utnapishtim built an ark and saved himself, his family and the beasts who inhabit the earth.

UTTU—*Sumer*

Daughter of Enki and Nindurra. Goddess of clothing.

XXII

VAINAMOINEN, VILA AND THE VOICES OF THE VOID

VAHAGN—*Armenia*
God of fire.

VAHRAN—*aka* Verethraghna—*Persia*
The god of sacred fire. He is able to assume nine forms. They are: a bird, a camel, a wild goat, a white horse, a warrior of the mortal persuasion, a boar, a handsome human youth, a bull and a ram.

VAINAMOINEN—*Finland*
A great sorceror who adeptly aided in Creation. He also invented the zither and is an accomplished

musician. His playing entrances all who hear it. A single tune from Vainamoinen tames fierce beasts and raging storms and brings peace to the entire world.

VAIROCANA—*India*

King of the demons. Mortals have unfortunate ideas about demons. Vairocana is a lawful individual whose only desire is to do his job well.

VAISRAVANA—*India*

God of wealth.

VALHALLA—*German*

The home of Odin. It is large, because it must accommodate a great many inhabitants, but it is not ostentatious. The roof is simply constructed of shields and it has 540 entrances, each wide enough to permit 800 heroes to march through side by side.

VALI—*German*

Son of Odin. He has not yet been born.

VALKYRIES—*dba* Idisi—*German*

Some of the Battle Maidens were once mortal but many of them were divinities in their own right before they assumed their current positions. They ride their horses through the air while dressed in full armor as befits those who lead heroes in battle. The points of each Valkyrie spear scatter brilliant sparks of light. When heroes fall in battle, one of the Valkyries leads the hero to Valhalla and offers him the Drinking Horn.

VARUNA—*India*

God of the sea. Creator of the world. Ruler of the universe.

VAYU—*Persia*

An assistant of Vohu Manah of the Amesha Spentas. Vayu helps the souls of just mortals surmount any obstacles during the journey they must make after death.

VAYU—*India*

Father of Hanuman. God of the wind.

VAZIMBA—*Madagascar*

The spirits of those who lived on the island of Madagascar before mortals came. Spiritually, it is a very powerful race.

VEJAMAT—*Latvia*

Goddess of the wind.

VELE—*Prussia*

Spirits of the waters and woods.

VELEDA—*German*

A great prophetess who is widely respected and consulted by many mortals.

VENUS—*Roman*

Daughter of Jupiter and Dione. However, Venus much prefers the tale that she was created by Uranus from the foam of the sea at the moment of his death. It's ever so much more romantic. Wife of Vulcan. Mother of Cupid, Hymen, Priapus and Aeneas. Goddess of love. Goddess of beauty. Goddess of fertility.

VERETHRAGHNA—*dba* Vahran—*Persia*

God of war. God of Vrahran Fire. Vrahran Fire is the most sacred of all fires. It is made of a combination of 16 fires, most of which belong to those in the metalworking trades.

VERTIMNUS—*aka* Vortumnus—*Roman*

God of buying and selling. God of the changing seasons.

VESNA—*Slav*

Goddess of spring.

VESTA—*Roman*

Virgin goddess of fire. Her handmaidens were called the King's Daughters and were treated as such. It was the sacred obligation of these Vestal Virgins to keep the holy fires burning upon the royal hearth.

VICTORIA—*Roman*

Goddess of victory.

VIDAR—*German*

Son of Odin. When the Aesir gods of Germany die, it will be Vidar's task to slay Fenrir the Wolf (*qv*). This task completed, he will be named a god in the new world.

VILA—*Slav*

The female spirits of the forests, clouds and mountains who protect national heroes. They are long-haired and winged and are quite beautiful. They are capable of calling forth whirlwinds, hailstorms and rain. They possess eternal youth.

VIRACOCHA—*Inca*

Supreme god. God of law. He sculpted in stone all the races of men and his work can still be seen today, much to the bafflement of archeologists.

VISHNU—*aka* Hari, Vikramaditya, Narayana, Ananta, Yajnesvara, Janardana, Kesava, Madhava, etc.—*India*

Husband of Bhu and Lakshmi. God of the sun. Protector of worlds. He is blue-skinned and has four hands. He and Lakshmi currently reside in Vaikuntha, where he keeps an eye on what is happening in the universe.

VODU—*Fon, Africa*

There are four families of the Vodu gods. They are: the sky gods, the earth gods, the thunder gods and the fate gods.

VOICE OF THE VOID—*Bambara, Africa*

Parent of Pembo, god of water, wisdom and agriculture, and his wife, Musso Koroni, goddess of disorder. The Voice of the Void is composed of the worlds and whirlwinds which forever spiral upward in creation and speak to those who listen.

VOLOS—*aka* Veles—*Slav*

God of the herd. God of cattle. God of prosperity. God of commerce.

VOLSUNG—*German*

The great-grandson of Odin.

VOLTAN—*Maya*

God of Earth.

VOSEGUS—*Gaul*

God of the Vosges Forest.

VRITRA—*India*

A demon who became known as the Great Obstructor.

VULCAN—*Roman*

Son of Jupiter and Juno. Husband of Maia and Venus. God of fire. God of volcanoes. The manufacturer of art, arms and armor for gods and heroes alike. Workmanship, excellent. An example is the construction of the famed thunderbolts of Jupiter which are as good today as the day they were forged. He was lamed in a fall at home but he is quite strong and powerful due to his work at the smithy.

XXIII

THE WAKAN-TANKA

WAK—*Hamitic*

God of the sky. He is worshipped chiefly by the Orma, or Sons of Men, of Africa. The Orma are called the Galla by others.

WAKAN-TANKA—*Sioux Indian*

A collective unity of the gods which has tremendous power. It is much like a gathering of world leaders, but it is not as ineffective. As a matter of fact, it is highly effective.

WALPURGISNACHT—*German*

The night of April 30, or Beltane Eve. It is the beginning of the growing season and, on this date, area witches assemble to pray that the gods will bless the crops and bring fertility.

WAMARA—*Baziba, Africa*
Son of Nyante. Father of Kagoro, Mugasba, Kazoba and Ryangombe.

WANTU SU—*Sudan*
The supreme god.

WATI and KUTJARA—*Australia*
The two male ancestors of mortals who taught them to keep in touch with Dreamtime. Dreamtime is always present and is the source of all life.

WINDIGO—*aka* Whitiko, Weendigo, Witigo and Wehtiko—*Ojibwa, Chippewa and Algonquin Indian*
A race of giant cannibals who prey upon human beings in the winter when food is scarce. Quite apart from their size, these creatures have twisted mouths, emaciated bodies and hearts of ice. They emit a series of eerie whistles and also roar loudly. The only known way to destroy a Windigo is to hack it to pieces and burn it to melt its heart. Otherwise, it is liable to come back to life, hungrier than before.

WITCH
Female priest.

WOTO—*aka* Oto—*Shongo, Africa*
God of fire.

WULUWAID—*Australia*
A male rainmaker.

XXIV

XEVIOSO OF VODU

XANTHUS and BALIUS—*Greek*
Offspring of Zephyrus and Podarge the Harpie. This superb matched pair of horses are immortal and endowed with human speech. Their swiftness and intelligence led them to seek service as chariot horses to Achilles during the Trojan War.

XEVIOSO—*Fon, Africa*
Son of Mahu and Lisa. Twin of Gun. A member of the Vodu gods. God of thunder.

XIPE TOTEC—*Aztec*
God of spring. God of renewal. God of flowers. God of vegetation.

XIUHTECUHTLI—*aka* Huehueteotl—*Aztec*
God of fire.

XOCHIPILLI—*Mexico*
Husband of Xochiquetzal. God of flowers. God of sport. God of dance. God of games. God of beauty. God of love. God of youth.

XOLOTL—*Aztec*
Brother of Quetzalcoatl. God of monsters. God of magicians. God of twins. God of double ears of maize.

XXV

YAHWEH, YEMANJA AND YGGDRASIL

YAHWEH—*Semite*

Storm god. By all accounts, he is an extremely jealous god who cannot tolerate the presence of other divinities. This is a source of great puzzlement to many of them as, when Yahweh was a member of the Grand Council of the Gods presided over by El of Ugarit, relations between Yahweh and the rest of the council members were always most cordial.

YAMA—*India*

Brother-husband of his twin sister Yami. Creator of the human race. God of the dead. The Yamadutas bring him the souls of the dead. He has an odd greenish complexion and is a bit heavyset. Currently resides in Yamapura.

YAMA-NO-KAMI—*Japan*
Goddess of the hunt. Goddess of the forest. Goddess of agriculture. Goddess of vegetation.

YAMM—*Ugarit*
A god of the sea.

YANGOMBI—*Bantu, Africa*
God of creation.

YAROVIT—*Slav*
God of victory.

YAYU—*India*
God of air.

YEMANJA—*Brazil*
Goddess of the sea. On New Year's Eve, at midnight, those who love Yemanja go to a beach and light a candle in her name. Then, little boats constructed of flowers are set adrift on the waves. If they are taken out to the sea by Yemanja, a good year will come. If they are refused and thrown back onto the sand, it will be a bad year.

YEMAYA—*Africa, Central America, the Caribbean*
God of the deep sea.

YEN-LO-WANG—*China*
God of Earth.

YGGDRASIL—*German*
The ash tree whose branches are spread over the entire world. It connects all parts of the universe, as

well as the past, the present and the future. It has three main roots. One root is in Asgard and extends deep into Urd's well, the fountain of youth. One root is in Niflheim, where it enters Hrergelmir's fountain, which is the source of the great rivers of the world. The third root is in Jotunheim's Fountain of Mirmir, the fountain of wisdom. Yggdrasil suffers great anguish, as its roots are always being gnawed by serpents and its leaves eaten by deer. It was also forced to serve as gallows when Odin hung nine days in sacrifice. Nevertheless, Yggdrasil persists. It supports the universe, you see, and it must survive.

YI—*China*
Husband of Chang-o. He saved the earth from destruction when all ten of its suns appeared in the sky at the same time. Yi, an expert archer with a magic bow, shot down nine of the suns.

YIMA—*Persia*
God of light. He is responsible for the fact that the earth is three times larger than originally intended. Mortal humans and mortal animals have overpopulated the planet three times and each time. Yima has enlarged it for them.

YMIR—*German*
Father of the Race of Giants. His body was formed from Eternal Ice, which was melted and quickened to life by air from the Fires of the South. Ymir then created giants, gods and mortals.

YNAKHSYT—*Yakut (Siberia)*
Goddess of cattle.

YU HUANG—*dba* The Jade God—*China*

Son of Pao Yu and Ching Te. Emperor of the Gods. God of purity. God of nature. All the lesser gods report to him on human activities.

YU-CH'IANG—*China*

God of the sea wind. He may go about disguised as a giant sea bird or a whale, but he always has the face, hands and feet of a human male.

XXVI

ZABA TO ZVORUNA AND THE 115 MISTRESSES OF ZEUS

ZABA—*Hurrite*
God of war.

ZABABA—*Kish*
God of gods.

ZAGREUS—*dba* Iacchus—*Greek*
Son of Zeus and Persephone. God of rebirth. God of immortality. When Hera discovered that Persephone had borne Zeus a son, she was furious. She ordered the Titans to dispose of the child. They cut him to pieces and ate him. Zeus snatched the child's

still-beating heart and, from this, regenerated his son. He renamed the child Iacchus and told Hera that since Zagreus was officially dead she had best consider the entire matter settled once and for all.

ZAM—*Persia*
An earth-spirit.

ZANAHARY—*aka ZANAHARIBE—Madagascar*
The Zanahary sky-gods created the human race.

ZARATHUSTRA—*Persia*
A powerful priest-magician who speaks with the gods, frustrates the schemes of demons and performs miracles.

ZATAVU—*Madagascar*
A great magician. He won the hand of a Zanahary sky-princess in marriage. The Zanahary scorned his request, stating that mortals were creatures of Zanahary making and such a union was improper. However, Zatavu was able to prove to the Zanahary that he created himself. So strong was his logic that they had no choice but to agree to the marriage.

ZAZAVAVINDRANO—*Madagascar*
Water spirits. Mortal males claim that there is nothing a Zazavavindrano wants more than to marry a mortal male. That is not what the Zazavavindrano say.

ZEMPAT—*Prussia*
God of the earth. God of cattle.

ZEPHYRUS—*Greek*
Son of Astraeus and Eos. Brother of Chloris, Iris and Podarge. Father of Carpus, Xanthus and Balius. God of the west wind. Winged horse.

ZEUS—*Greek*

Son of Cronus and Rhea. Brother of Hestia, Demeter, Hades and Poseidon. Brother-husband of Hera. Husband of Metis, Themis, Eurynome, Mnemosyne, Demeter, Letu and Maia. Also has over 115 mistresses (some mortal) and 140 children. Divine children include Dionysus, Apollo, Hermes, Ares, Artemis, Hebe, Athena and Hephaestus. Father of Gods and mortals. Master of destiny. God of the sky. God of weather. Protector of guests. Guardian of law and upholder of morality. Given his amorous tendencies, the latter bespeaks a certain contradiction in Zeus's almighty nature. However, as he is armed with the thunder and lightning, it is impolitic to raise this point.

ZINKIBARU—*Songhoi, Africa*

A djinn. Although he is blind, he is the Master of Fish.

ZIVA—*aka* Siva—*Slav*

Goddess of life.

ZOMBIE—*Caribbean*

A reanimated corpse. Zombies can be employed as drudges but are poor workers. Feeding salt to a zombie counteracts the spell, which then cannot be worked again on that particular corpse.

ZU—*aka* Imdugud—*Assyria*

God of thunder. God of storms.

ZURVAN—*Persia*

Father of Ahriman and Ohrmazd; he had to offer sacrifices for 1,000 years to get them because he is androgynous. God of infinite time.

ZVORUNA—*Lithuania*

Goddess of the hunt. Goddess of animals.

ABOUT THE AUTHOR

ANNE SCHERGER BAUMGARTNER is the editor of *The Miami Herald's* Action Line column and a graduate of Ohio University. She and her husband Gary, both avid sailors, call Coconut Grove, Florida, home. They are owned by several cats.

Her interest in mythology dates from her kindergarten days when she was severely chastised by her teacher for telling classmates a fantastic story of a great winged horse which would carry her across the sea. The Baumgartners' sailboat is named Pegasus.